BUTTER

AND

INSECTS

PAUL STERRY

HAMLYN

HOW TO USE THIS BOOK

LIME HAWK MOTH
Mimas tiliae
W 65mm. Wings resemble
dry leaves. Larvae feed
on lime.

This guide covers over 200 species of
insect, most of which are likely to be seen
in the UK. The identification pages (44-
125) give the common English name
(except for those species which do not
have a distinguishing common English
name), followed by the scientific name in
italics. Length (L) or wingspan (W) are in
millimetres, and some additional useful
information, such as habitat or habits,
is given. On the butterfly pages, the
upperside of the wing is shown on the left,
the underside on the right; ♂ means
male, ♀ means female. For moths, adult
males are illustrated, and, wherever
possible, the characteristic resting
position is shown also.

ACKNOWLEDGEMENTS

The author and publishers would like to thank the
following individuals for their assistance in the
preparation of this book: Andrew Branson of British
Wildlife Publishing, Principal Consultant · David
Christie, Editorial Consultant · and Derek Hall, who
conceived the series.

Published in 1991 by
Hamlyn Children's Books,
part of Reed International Books,
Michelin House, 81 Fulham Road,
London SW3 6RB

ISBN 0 600 56950 0

Printed in Portugal

CONTENTS

INSECT CHARACTERISTICS

Insects are an extremely varied group of animals. The smallest are only a few millimetres long while the largest may be 20cm or more in length. They come in all shapes, sizes and colours, but they all have certain characteristics in common which tell us they are insects. Adult insects have a body divided into three main sections: the head, the thorax and the abdomen. The head bears the eyes, mouthparts and two antennae. To the thorax are attached two pairs of wings and three pairs of legs. The abdomen, containing the digestive and reproductive organs, is usually segmented.

Insects are the only group of invertebrates – animals without backbones – that can fly. The membranous wings are attached to the abdomen and are moved using internal muscles. Some insects can fly for long distances.

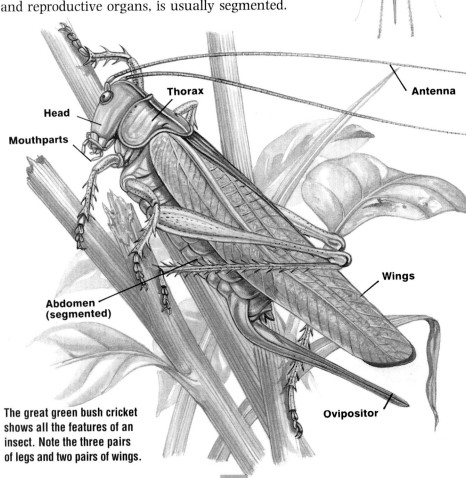

Thorax

Head

Mouthparts

Antenna

Wings

Abdomen (segmented)

Ovipositor

The great green bush cricket shows all the features of an insect. Note the three pairs of legs and two pairs of wings.

Like other insects, dragonflies have two pairs of wings. These are membranous and transparent. The veins – which are used to help pump up the wings after the insect has metamorphosed – can be seen. It is easy to see where the wings are attached to the upper surface of the abdomen. Dragonflies are superb fliers and can even hover in mid-air. They catch small insects in flight and eat them on the wing.

In common with many other beetles, the violet ground beetle has powerful, biting mouthparts. The sharp mandibles help it to chew through the tough skin of other insects. The palps are sensory organs which help it to detect its food and the environment around it. Its compound eyes on the sides of its head also locate food and danger. The beetle's head and body are well armoured.

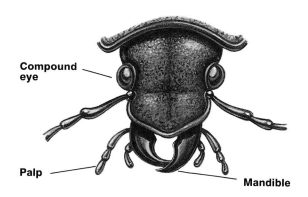

Compound eye

Palp

Mandible

PROJECT

Look closely at an insect. The outside of an insect's body is hard and is made of a substance known as chitin. This protects the soft inside of the animal from damage. This exoskeleton, as it is called, also supports the body in the same way as bones support our bodies. In order to move, the insect has flexible joints between different parts of the body. These joints are most easily seen on the legs. The muscles are attached to the inside of the exoskeleton. Many schools keep insects for study, such as this praying mantis, so are good places to watch how an insect's body moves.

STRUCTURE AND MOULT

The bodies of insects are complex and differ greatly from our own. They do not have lungs but breathe instead using a network of tubes called tracheae. These open to the air via holes called spiracles, which can be seen on the abdomen, one pair per segment. All the muscles that allow the insect to walk, hop or fly are inside the body as well. They attach to the inside of the exoskeleton. The gut runs through the length of the body, but most of the digestive and reproductive organs are in the abdomen. There are only a few true blood vessels: most of the blood lies in cavities surrounding the tissues.

Moulting
An insect's outer skin is tough and inflexible compared with our skin which is soft. Although its skin can expand a little bit, it has to shed it if it wants to grow much larger. Shedding the skin is called moulting and most insects do it several times during their larval or nymphal stages. Just after moulting, the new skin is still soft, so the body can expand.

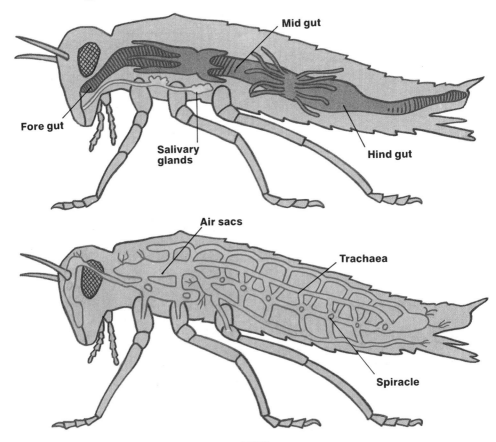

Mid gut

Fore gut

Salivary glands

Hind gut

Air sacs

Trachaea

Spiracle

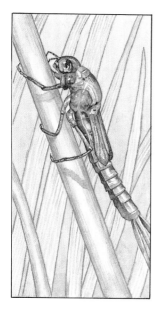

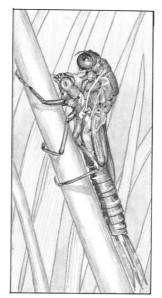

Metamorphosis
In the first stage of meta-
morphosis the damselfly
nymph climbs up a grass
stem. It pauses for a while to
get a firm grip. The pale body
of the adult can be seen
through the nymph's skin.

Next the nymphal skin splits
lengthways down the back of
the thorax. By considerable
effort the soft-bodied adult
pushes its head, thorax and
legs through this split. The
wings are tiny and shrivelled
at this stage.

After resting, the adult grips
the grass stem with its legs
and pulls the abdomen free
of the nymphal skin. The
wings are then pumped up to
their full size, after which
they set hard. The whole
process takes about an hour.

Adult insects see using
compound eyes. These are
best developed in
dragonflies (right) and flies.
Each eye consists of
hundreds of tiny cells, called
ommatidia, each of which
forms a small image. The
insect's brain combines the
images to give a full picture
of the world around it.

LIFE CYCLES

During their lives, insects go through different stages; these changes in shape and structure are called metamorphosis. In a butterfly's life cycle, all the stages – adult, egg, larva and pupa – look very different from each other. The wings appear only in the adult, and metamorphosis is very noticeable. With grasshoppers, however, the young 'nymph' looks rather like a miniature adult, becoming more so as it grows and moults. The wings appear gradually and metamorphosis does not involve dramatic change in structure or shape.

With most adult moths, it is possible to tell females from males. Sometimes they are different in size or colour. Their pupae also look different. Compare the markings on the tip of the abdomen with those shown above.

The swallowtail's egg is laid on its foodplant. The caterpillar hatches after 10–12 days.

Butterfly
Adult butterflies have two pairs of wings, which are covered in tiny scales and are usually colourful.

The swallowtail butterfly is a beautiful species named after the streamers on its hindwings. It lives in marshy areas where its foodplant, milk parsley, grows. The long tongue is used to drink nectar from flowers.

The pupa is attached to a plant stem. It is held securely by a silk thread.

The caterpillars are brightly coloured to warn birds of their unpleasant taste.

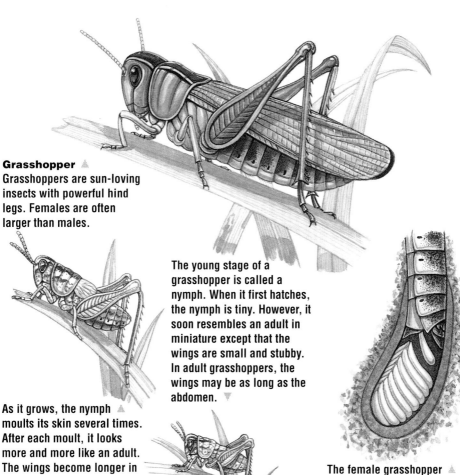

Grasshopper ⬙
Grasshoppers are sun-loving insects with powerful hind legs. Females are often larger than males.

The young stage of a grasshopper is called a nymph. When it first hatches, the nymph is tiny. However, it soon resembles an adult in miniature except that the wings are small and stubby. In adult grasshoppers, the wings may be as long as the abdomen. ▽

As it grows, the nymph ⬙ moults its skin several times. After each moult, it looks more and more like an adult. The wings become longer in relation to the body length.

The female grasshopper ⬙ uses her abdomen to lay eggs deep in the soil.

PROJECT

Although you can buy butterfly eggs, it is more fun to find them for yourself: search on leaves and twigs in spring and summer. When caterpillars hatch, give them fresh leaves of the correct foodplant each day and keep a sprig of leaves alive in water in a cage. Some species pupate on the foodplant, while others burrow in the soil. Provide both alternatives if you are not certain of your caterpillars' needs. Keep the pupae cool until they hatch.

FEEDING

Because insects are such a large and varied group of animals, it is not surprising that almost everything living is eaten by one species or another. There are herbivores (plant-eaters) that eat seeds, fruits, leaves and wood; and carnivores (meat-eaters) that catch other insects. Dragonfly nymphs can even kill small fish. Fungi and decaying plants and animals are also attacked, and some insects parasitise living animals. Perhaps the most significant way of feeding is found in the plant-eaters. Caterpillars and other insects that eat leaves cause damage to the plants, but many other insects – sometimes even the adult butterflies – actually benefit the plants by pollinating them.

Mouthparts
Insect mouthparts are among the most varied of any group of animals. There are biting, chewing and sucking mouthparts and some that are used to pierce either plant tissue or animal skin. If you look closely, however, all these different types of mouthparts have the same basic structure. A hard substance called chitin gives them their strength.

The convolvulus hawk moth has a long tongue to reach nectar. It picks up pollen and carries it to the next flower.

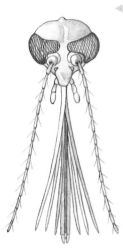

Female mosquitoes have sharp, piercing mouthparts which can easily penetrate human skin. A central canal allows blood to pass up the tube. They need a meal before they can lay fertile eggs. Excess blood is passed from the abdomen.

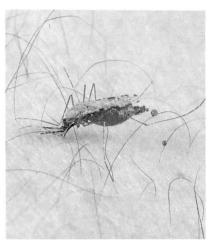

Flies have mouthparts ▼ which act like vacuum cleaners. When they settle on household food, they suck up the fluids, thereby taking in nutrients.

◀ Most beetles, such as the green tiger beetle, have powerful biting mouthparts. They catch other insects.

PROJECT

If you rear caterpillars from the egg stage through to the pupa, or chrysalis, it is interesting to watch their feeding habits. After they hatch, they are small and either graze the surface of the leaf or take tiny bites from the edges of young leaves. As they get bigger, they tackle larger leaves and take bigger and bigger bites. Watch how they use their legs and mouths to consume whole leaves systematically, strip by strip. Privet hawk moth caterpillars (right) make ideal subjects because they reach a large size by the time they pupate.

WINGS

Insects are the only group of invertebrates – animals without backbones – that can fly. However, it is only the adults that can do so, and not all species of insects have wings. There are usually two pairs of wings which are attached to the insect's thorax – the middle section of the body. Internal muscles make the wings beat and give the animal 'lift'. Flies use only one pair of wings to fly. The hind pair is reduced in size and helps with balance.

Butterfly wings are covered in overlapping tiny scales. In most species, they are brightly coloured and make distinctive patterns.

Unlike the buff-tailed bumble bee on the left, some insects do not have wings, even when they are adults. Fleas and silverfish are good examples. Most aphids (above) also lack wings. However, at certain times of year, aphids produce a generation of adults that do have wings. These then fly away and disperse.

The great prominent ⚠ moth's wings not only enable it to fly, but provide it with exceptional camouflage.

Caterpillars do not have ⚠ wings and cannot fly. Some species suspend themselves on silk threads to move or escape predators.

The way that insects fly varies from group to group. Hoverflies (top) beat their wings at a very fast rate and can hover perfectly. Butterflies, such as this white admiral (above), cannot hover but glide and flutter. Of course, butterfly caterpillars cannot fly. In stag beetles (right) the front pair of wings has become hardened to form a pair of protective wing cases. The true wings are underneath and unfold when the wing cases are lifted. A stag beetle's flight is weak.

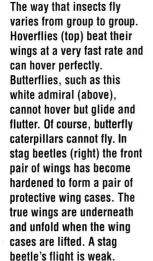

INSECT CLASSIFICATION

SILVERFISH
Order Thysanura.
Wingless. 3 tail filaments.

MAYFLIES
Order Ephemeroptera.
3 tail filaments, 2 pairs of unequal wings.

STONEFLIES
Order Plecoptera.
2 tail filaments, 2 pairs of unequal wings.

SPRINGTAILS
Order Collembola.
Wingless and tiny.
Forked spring.

BEES
Order Hymenoptera.
4 membranous wings, waisted body.

CLASSIFICATION

Although insects come in all shapes and sizes, and are extremely varied in the way they live, they can be sorted into groups with shared characteristics. Scientists working on classification have put all insects within the class Insecta, itself a division of the phylum Arthropoda, animals with jointed legs. Within insects, the largest sub-divisions are called orders; there are further sub-divisions called families, genera and species. A species is the smallest sub-division, and each has a scientific name of two words which are unique to it. With insects, the scientific name is important because many species do not have common English names, or only a general name, shared with other species.

WASPS
Order Hymenoptera.
2 pairs of unequal membranous wings.

BUTTERFLIES AND MOTHS
Order Lepidoptera.
Wings covered with scales.
Proboscis.

CADDISFLIES
Order Trichoptera.
2 pairs of unequal hairy wings.

TRUE FLIES
Order Diptera.
1 pair of functional wings.
2nd pair reduced.

SCORPION FLIES
Order Mecoptera.
Pronounced snout. Wings held flat.

DRAGONFLIES
Order Odonata.
2 pairs of equal wings and
long abdomen.

GRASSHOPPERS
Order Orthoptera.
Wings held over body. Large
hind legs.

EARWIGS
Order Dermaptera.
Pincers. Hindwings fold
under forewings.

COCKROACHES
Order Dictyoptera.
Flattened wings. 2 tail
filaments.

IDENTIFICATION

Although you may not be able to recognise
each species of insect as you see it, it
should be relatively easy, with practice, to
know to which order it belongs. Study
carefully this diagram of many of the main
orders and note the important features.
Before long you will know whether the
insect you have just found is a bug or a
beetle, or a caddisfly or a moth. Key
features to look for include the number of
functional (working) wings, and whether
they are clear or covered in scales or hair.
The shape and size of the antennae are also
important, as are any noticeable projections
from the body. Once you have decided what
order a specimen belongs to, you can then
try to identify its particular species.

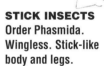

STICK INSECTS
Order Phasmida.
Wingless. Stick-like
body and legs.

LACEWINGS
Order Neuroptera.
Membranous wings held
roof-like at rest.

BEETLES
Order Coleoptera.
Hardened forewings cover
hindwings.

BUGS
Order Hemiptera.
Hardened forewings,
piercing mouthparts.

PRAYING MANTIDS
Order Dictyoptera.
Modified fore legs.
Flattened wings.

SIGNS AND SEARCHING

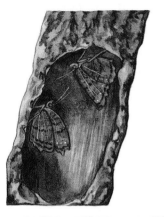

Hibernation
Peacock butterflies often hibernate in hollow trees. Search in cracks and crevices using a torch to help locate the insects.

Shelter ▶
The caterpillar of the red admiral spins silk threads to tie together the leaves of its foodplant – stinging nettle. This helps protect it.

◀ Hibernation
Small tortoiseshells often spend the winter hibernating indoors or in a shed or outhouse. Search in dark corners and under ledges to find them. The underwings are dark and so the butterfly is not conspicuous. Several may congregate together.

CAREFUL OBSERVATION

Finding insects can be difficult. Many of them hide and are difficult to spot, and some have superb camouflage. However, with a bit of careful detective work, you can soon find a surprising range of creatures that are normally well hidden. Knowing where to look helps enormously, so do some background reading to help find clues. For example, if you want to find hibernating butterflies, try looking in hollow trees or on ceilings and walls of lofts and sheds. Caterpillars are also a challenge to find without using a beating tray – look for signs of feeding. Make sure that you keep good notes about your findings and observations.

Digging for pupae ▽
Many moth caterpillars pupate in the ground. Try digging around the base of trees to see what you can find. You may have to dig down several inches.

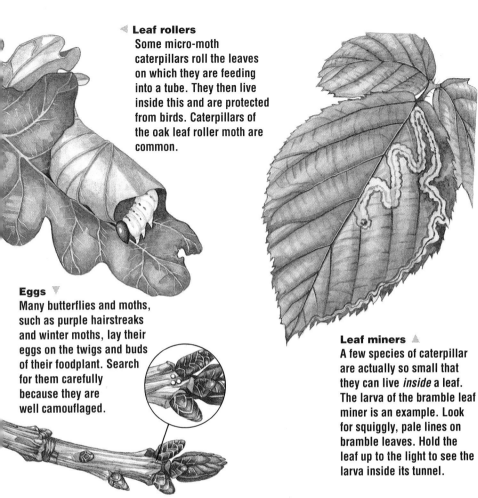

Leaf rollers

Some micro-moth caterpillars roll the leaves on which they are feeding into a tube. They then live inside this and are protected from birds. Caterpillars of the oak leaf roller moth are common.

Eggs

Many butterflies and moths, such as purple hairstreaks and winter moths, lay their eggs on the twigs and buds of their foodplant. Search for them carefully because they are well camouflaged.

Leaf miners

A few species of caterpillar are actually so small that they can live *inside* a leaf. The larva of the bramble leaf miner is an example. Look for squiggly, pale lines on bramble leaves. Hold the leaf up to the light to see the larva inside its tunnel.

PROJECT

Most of the larger galls that can be found in woods are caused by insects, although many people do not realise this. It is difficult to see the wasp, but the best way is to keep the gall at home and watch what emerges. Place the stem on which the gall is found in a jar of water in a cage. The best galls to use are those on oak, such as the oak apple or the marble gall (right). If there is a small, round hole in the gall, the wasp has already emerged. Use a rearing cage with a fine mesh because the gall wasps are very small.

NETTING AND CATCHING

Using a beating tray, or even a sheet laid on the ground, is a good technique for finding a variety of insects. Keep notes of where and when you find each species: are there more species on trees and bushes that are native to this country?

BEATING TRAYS

Many insects feed and hide on trees and bushes among the foliage. Vegetation can be extremely productive for caterpillars, beetles and bugs, but they are often difficult to spot because many of them are camouflaged. One of the best ways to find them is to use a beating tray; some people make do with an old umbrella. The tray, which is best made with white material so that the insects stand out, is held under a branch which is given a sharp tap with a stick. The insects fall off and land in the tray or umbrella, where they can be examined. Do not hit the branch with too much force and always put the insects back when you have finished with them.

After you have caught an insect in a net it is useful to examine it in a transparent pot. Hold the bag of the net upright and gently pot the insect from beneath to stop it escaping or being damaged.

Lots of tiny insects live in the soil and can be difficult to find. You may be lucky by turning over pieces of bark or logs. However, for better results try burying bundles of straws just below the surface of the soil. Small creatures will take refuge there and can easily be removed by blowing them out. The larger the bore of the tubing, the larger the insects that you will find.

Pit-fall and flip-top traps are another good way to catch beetles and other ground-dwelling insects. Bury a jar up to its rim in the soil and shelter the mouth with a piece of wood or a tile. This prevents water collecting in the bottom and drowning the insects. Place a twig in the jar to help shrews climb out and escape; and inspect the trap at least twice a day.

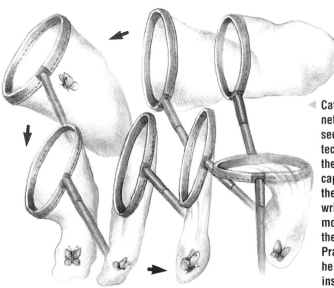

Catching a butterfly with a net is not as easy as it might seem. There is a definite technique to it. Having swept the net through the air and captured the butterfly, twist the net handle with your wrist. This closes off the mouth of the net and stops the insect escaping. Practising this method will help. Always release the insect unharmed.

ATTRACTING MOTHS

Using simple techniques, it is possible to attract many more moths than can be found by casual observation around lighted windows. It is important to choose the location carefully: near a hedge comprising several different plant species is a good spot, as is a meadow next to a woodland. Gardens are also often surprisingly productive. Be sure to keep a good record of your catch – write the details in a notebook.

Moth treacle
Coat a tree trunk or wooden fence with a sugary mixture of 2 tablespoons of treacle, 1 tablespoon of beer and 2 tablespoons of sugar. Between sunset and midnight, on warm summer evenings, are the best times for this method.

Plants
Moths feed on nectar-rich plants in the same way as butterflies do. Watch around plants such as honeysuckle (above), stinging nettles, cow parsley and ragwort. Most moth species prefer native plants.

Moth trap ▷
A mercury-vapour lamp is the most efficient moth attractor. The bulb gives off ultraviolet light, to which moths are more responsive than white light.

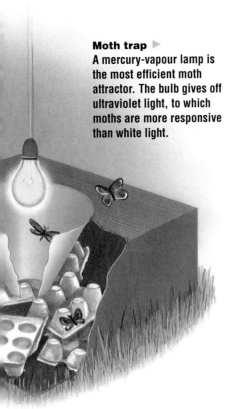

Moth trap △
Moth traps are expensive to buy but can be made using a wooden box, a funnel and a bulb. If you are using a proper moth trap, fill the base with old cardboard egg trays. The moths can settle and rest on these.

Light ▷
Ordinary white light will always attract a few moths. Try shining a bright torch or light bulb on an extension lead on to a white sheet suspended between two posts. Moths can be seen in your garden by examining flowers after dark with a hand-held torch.

REARING INSECTS

Observing the life cycles of insects is very rewarding. Many caterpillars have curious shapes and beautiful colours and are worth studying in themselves. The eggs may be delicately sculptured and the pupae attractively marked. It is fun to follow the whole process with the insect in captivity. You do not need expensive equipment in order to do this. You can try 'sleeving' caterpillars on their foodplant. Take a piece of muslin or fine net and sew two edges to make a tube. Slip this over a branch and tie at each end with the caterpillars inside. They then will always have fresh food whenever they need it.

When rearing caterpillars from the egg stage, let them eat their egg shells if they want to. They may need them to get essential nutrients.

The easiest way of confining caterpillars to a foodplant which is still growing is by sleeving. Easily-grown foodplants can be potted and placed in a rearing cage.

To watch dragonflies emerge from their nymphs, collect a few nymphs in May and June and place them in a bucket with water and weed and pond animals (below). The nymphs need twigs to climb up before they can metamorphose. Caterpillars can be reared on living plants in larvae cylinders (right). The plant is grown in a pot or kept in water. A gauze base and metal lid prevent the caterpillar escaping from the cylinder.

FIELD NOTES

MAKING NOTES

It is a good idea to make notes of what you see on a day out. It can be extremely useful if you are uncertain of an insect's identity. If you keep your notebooks, you may also be able to spot trends in insect abundance and relate their appearance to weather conditions or time of year. Try sketching the outline of the insect. If it is a butterfly, fill in the colours and note the approximate size. You should also note the date, time of day, weather, habitat, what it was feeding on, and habits, to help with its identification when you get home.

Make a note and sketch of any interesting behaviour. For example, male speckled woods fight in spiral flight in woodland glades.

Young caterpillars are ▼ often rather delicate. If you are removing one from its foodplant in order to identify it, use a paintbrush to avoid harming it.

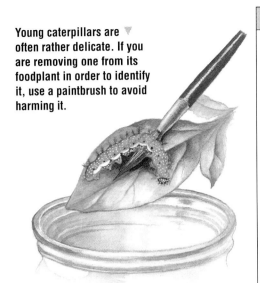

When you are studying caterpillars, note what they are eating – this is a death's head hawk moth caterpillar on potato. You will then know what food to give them if you are rearing them. It is also an identification point: some species only eat one type of plant.

Take care when you study ▼ grasshoppers: they can shed their back legs if they are not handled properly.

◁ If you want to examine a grasshopper closely do not be tempted to pick it up. Instead, place the mouth of a clear tube near its head and encourage it to crawl in. Having examined it in detail, you can then let it go unharmed.

HOW TO WATCH

With a few insects, it may be difficult even to work out which group they belong to. Try to learn all the key features so that you know what to look for and what to note down. For instance, with this insect you should note the length of the antennae, the presence of an ovipositor, the long hind legs and the colour: it is a female speckled bush cricket.

PHOTOGRAPHY

In the past, entomologists – people who study insects – caught and killed insects, storing their pinned specimens in large boxes. This was the only way they had to record their studies. Nowadays, naturalists are more fortunate. Modern cameras are easy to use and have lenses which allow close-up photographs to be taken. With practice, anyone can take beautiful pictures, and these are a much better way to record butterflies, moths and other insects than pinning dead specimens. The photos provide hours of pleasure and can be shown to friends.

A single-lens reflex camera (SLR) is the best type for wildlife photography. A mirror within the camera body allows you to see the exact image that will appear on your photograph. Just before the shutter opens, the mirror swings out of the way. A macro lens allows close focusing.

Butterflies love to drink nectar from flowers. Small tortoiseshells are especially fond of garden flowers such as buddleia and ice-plant. The best way to get a photograph is to set your camera up, focused on a flower. Do not stalk the butterfly, but wait for it to come to you.

Many insects do not stay still for  very long. Because the light from a flashgun lasts only a fraction of a second, use it to help 'freeze' any movement. Having flashguns on both sides of the camera softens dark shadows and creates a more natural photograph. Mount the camera on a tripod or monopod.

Grasshoppers are sun-loving insects. In the heat of the day they hop or fly at the slightest disturbance. Like many butterflies, they are most easy to approach as they warm up in the mornings.

Some species of  butterfly, such as blues and coppers, like to sunbathe. Photograph them early in the morning or in the late afternoon when they are least active. In the mornings, they need the sun to become active; and, in the evenings, they bask in the sunshine.

Not all moths fly at night. The emperor is a large day-flying moth which can be seen on heaths and moors. The females attract the males with a special smell, and sooner or later males will appear. They are often distracted by the female and are easy to photograph.

TAKING GOOD PHOTOGRAPHS

1. Use a film with a speed between 64 and 200 ASA. Kodak, Fuji and Agfa are good.
2. For close-up photography, use a tripod. This keeps the camera steady and lets you use a small lens aperture and hence gives a good depth of field.
3. Avoid sudden movements which may frighten your photographic subject.
4. Try to frame the insect in the middle of the picture. With butterflies, keep the wings parallel to the film plane. In this way, more of the subject will be in focus.

DECIDUOUS WOODLAND

Woodlands are wonderful habitats for the study of insects. Insects abound, and there is always something to look for, even in the dead of winter. Deciduous woodlands – woods whose trees shed their leaves in winter – are especially rich in insect life. Caterpillars attack the leaves in the summer months, and moths and beetles hide among the bark and leaf litter on the woodland floor. In summer, sunny woodland clearings encourage a luxuriant growth of flowers, which attract butterflies.

Oak leaf roller ▲
The caterpillar lives inside a rolled-up leaf and suspends itself by a silk thread when threatened or alarmed.

Comma ▼
Comma butterflies hibernate during the winter; you can see them in the spring and the autumn.

Purple hairstreak ▲
These colourful butterflies live in colonies in the canopy of oak trees. On sunny days, they fly near the tree tops.

Hoverfly ◄
Some species of hoverfly have markings similar to wasps and bees. They feed on flowers in sunny woodland clearings.

White admiral ▲
White admiral butterflies live in old oak woods and lay their eggs on honeysuckle leaves. They are fond of bramble flowers.

Mottled umber ▶
This moth caterpillar has beautiful markings. It walks by 'looping-the-loop'. When still it resembles a twig.

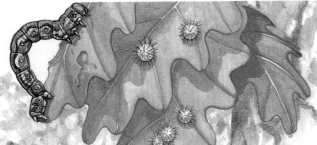

◀ Purple emperor
This impressive butterfly lives in oak woods and lays its eggs on sallow. The males have a purple sheen.

Spangle galls ▲
These curious little galls are common on the underside of oak leaves. They are caused by a tiny wasp.

▼ Speckled wood
Male speckled wood butterflies guard a territory in a sunny clearing and fight intruders.

◀ Stag beetle
Male stag beetles fight for the right to mate with a female. They use their large, antler-like mandibles to dislodge each other.

Mottled umber ▶
This moth is superbly camouflaged as it rests on tree bark, protecting it from birds.

Wood cricket ▶
These engaging little insects live among piles of leaf litter in a few old woodlands.

CONIFEROUS WOODLAND

Coniferous woodlands – ones where the trees keep their leaves throughout the year – are generally not so productive as deciduous woodlands. The trees may not be native to the country, and so many of our insects may not like to feed on them. However, there is still plenty to look for. Wood ants build large colonial nest mounds and butterflies fly along the woodland rides. Sawflies can be common, and several species of moth rest on the bark.

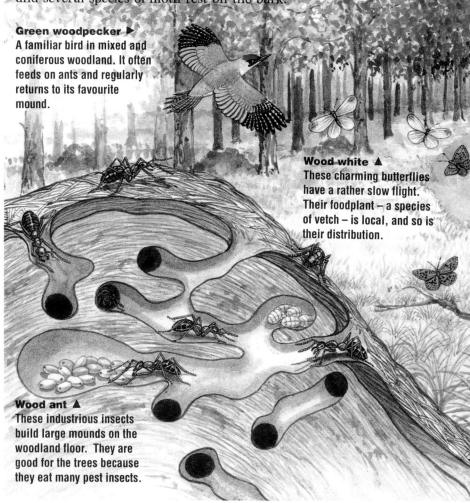

Green woodpecker ▶
A familiar bird in mixed and coniferous woodland. It often feeds on ants and regularly returns to its favourite mound.

Wood white ▲
These charming butterflies have a rather slow flight. Their foodplant – a species of vetch – is local, and so is their distribution.

Wood ant ▲
These industrious insects build large mounds on the woodland floor. They are good for the trees because they eat many pest insects.

PROJECT

Chrysalids are the pupae of moths and butterflies. Many species change from caterpillar to chrysalis after they have burrowed underground for safety. In pine woodlands, the pupae are usually found close to tree trunks. It is here that the caterpillar would have burrowed after climbing down the tree. Use a trowel gently to dig the soil and pine needles. Return disturbed soil to the holes.

◄ Pine sawfly and larvae ▼
The pine sawfly's larvae are a serious forest pest, feeding on pine needles.

Pine hawk moth larvae ▼
These caterpillars are beautifully marked and closely resemble the pine needles on which they feed.

Wood wasp ►
This large and fearsome species of sawfly lays its eggs in pine wood, using its needle-like ovipositor.

Pine hawk moth ►
Although this is a large species, it shows superb camouflage when at rest.

▼ Ladybird
Ladybirds are also the woodman's friend – they and their larvae eat pest insects. They often hibernate among log piles.

HEDGEROWS

Hedgerows are good habitats because many different species of shrubs and bushes grow in them. Wild flowers are often seen in abundance, too. The variety of vegetation encourages many different types of insect. Flowers of bramble and hogweed attract butterflies, hoverflies and beetles. Moths lay their eggs on the leaves, and bush crickets crawl and hop among the foliage. Because woods are being destroyed, hedgerows are an important refuge for woodland wildlife.

Scorpion fly ▲
The tip of the abdomen in males is like a scorpion's tail. They feed on insects caught in spiders' webs.

Gatekeeper ▲
These active butterflies are fond of bramble patches. Their caterpillars feed on grasses. They are common in summer.

Bumble bee ▶
Bumble bees visit flowers to collect the pollen and feed on nectar. They make their nests in old mouse-burrows.

Lappet moth caterpillar
This is one of the largest British caterpillars. It is extremely hairy and well camouflaged as it rests on twigs of hawthorn. It wanders before it pupates.

Hawthorn shieldbug
These are easiest to find in the autumn, when they feed on hawthorn berries.

Lappet moth
The shape and colour of the wings are a perfect match for dead leaves. The moth is very difficult to spot as it rests among the foliage.

Dark bush cricket
This species is very common among bramble patches. The males have a short, chirping song. They are very alert.

Aphid
These tiny insects feed by sucking plant sap. Generally they are found in large colonies.

Red admiral
This colourful butterfly is seen in the summer months. The eggs are laid on nettles. The caterpillars have very spiny hairs.

MEADOWS

The recent loss of many meadows to agricultural and urban development has destroyed one of the richest habitats for insects. In meadows grasses are abundant and there is usually a rich variety of colourful flowers. These provide food for both adult and larval insects. Butterflies are often abundant. Skippers and species of 'brown' butterflies – family Satyridae – are especially common because their caterpillars feed on grass leaves. Hoverflies and beetles are also numerous on flower heads.

Common blue ▼
Common blues are numerous in meadows where their foodplant, bird's-foot trefoil, grows. Mating pairs rest on grass heads.

◄ Small skipper
These are active little butterflies that have a buzzing flight. At rest, the wings are held slightly apart.

Six-spot burnet moth ►
This day-flying moth mates beside a yellowish cocoon attached to a grass stem. It likes flowers of knapweeds.

Ladybird ►
Ladybirds fly in warm weather. Both adults and their larvae feed on aphids. They are usually common on dock plants.

Cuckoo spit and froghopper ▲
The young froghopper – called a nymph – lives in a frothy mass which protects it from predators.

Bumble bee ▲
The bumble bee visits flowers to collect nectar and pollen. Queen bees hibernate and are most active in spring.

◄ Meadow brown
Abundant in most meadows, the meadow brown is constantly active in search of flowers such as bramble and hogweed.

Hoverfly ▲
Many species mimic wasps, with black and yellow markings. They are seen feeding on flower heads.

▲ Meadow grasshopper
Meadow grasshoppers are common almost everywhere. Males often sing from bare patches of soil.

◄ Ringlet
Mating pairs are found in July and August. They rest on grass stems with their wings closed. The larvae feed at night on grass leaves.

THE COAST

Although insects have not colonised the sea itself, coastal land is nevertheless a good area to search for them. The sea tends to moderate the harshest extremes of winter and so many insects with a more southern distribution thrive only around the coast. Several species of bush cricket and grasshopper show this restricted distribution. Coastal areas – particularly those bordering the English Channel – are good areas to search for migrant insects. Newly arrived moths and butterflies, for example, often linger for several days within a few miles of the sea.

Silver-Y moth ▼
This is a common migrant species which can occur in considerable numbers in good years. It often spreads far inland by the end of the summer. It flies by day but also comes to moth traps and lighted windows.

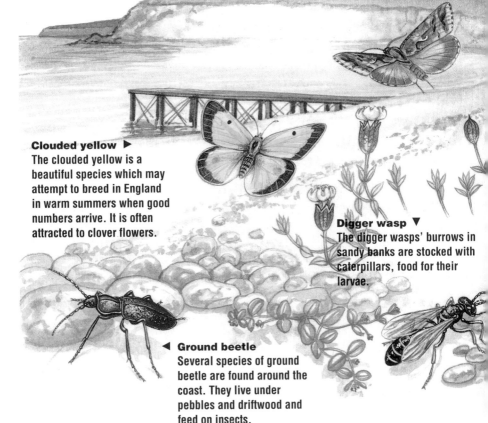

Clouded yellow ▶
The clouded yellow is a beautiful species which may attempt to breed in England in warm summers when good numbers arrive. It is often attracted to clover flowers.

Digger wasp ▼
The digger wasps' burrows in sandy banks are stocked with caterpillars, food for their larvae.

◀ Ground beetle
Several species of ground beetle are found around the coast. They live under pebbles and driftwood and feed on insects.

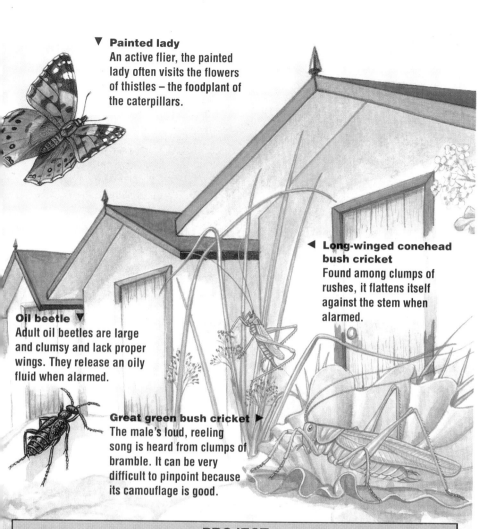

▼ Painted lady
An active flier, the painted lady often visits the flowers of thistles – the foodplant of the caterpillars.

◄ Long-winged conehead bush cricket
Found among clumps of rushes, it flattens itself against the stem when alarmed.

Oil beetle ▼
Adult oil beetles are large and clumsy and lack proper wings. They release an oily fluid when alarmed.

Great green bush cricket ►
The male's loud, reeling song is heard from clumps of bramble. It can be very difficult to pinpoint because its camouflage is good.

PROJECT

Some of our most spectacular moths, for example the death's head hawk moth (right) and the convolvulus hawk moth, are regular migrants to northern Europe in small numbers. They are best searched for around the coast – on fences, walls or beach huts, for example. They usually rest in the shade during the daytime and take to the wing at dusk to feed on flowers. Hummingbird hawk moths, on the other hand, are day-flying migrants that feed on the wing.

HEATHLAND AND MOORLAND

Both these habitats are found on acid soils and have their own special plants and animals. Heathlands are found in lowland Britain and Europe – usually on sandy soils – while moorlands are areas of upland. Typical plants include several species of heather and gorse, and the insects are adapted to feed on and live amongst this vegetation. Occasionally, areas of wet bogs develop, again with their own specialised plants and animals. Dragonflies and damselflies are conspicuous insects of heath and moor. They breed in pools and bogs.

Silver-studded blue ▼
Locally common on heathlands, this butterfly is very active on warm days.

▼ Four-spot libellula
This is an extremely active species that catches flies and midges on the wing. It often patrols a territory from a regular look-out post.

▼ Mining bee
Smaller but similar in size and shape to the honey bee, this bee digs its nest in dry, sandy banks.

◄ Gorse shieldbug
Often found in large groups on sprays of gorse, the preferred host plant. It hibernates in winter.

Bog bush cricket ►
This is a common heathland species, but usually only in wetter areas where cross-leaved heath grows. It is easily disturbed.

◄ Dusky cockroach
The dusky cockroach is extremely active among the low vegetation and easily overlooked.

Grayling ▼

At rest, the grayling shows remarkable camouflage on the bare heathland soil. It even orientates its wings towards the sun so that they cast the minimum amount of shadow. It is common in lowland areas.

PROJECT

Search for our largest grasshopper, the large marsh grasshopper. It is found on boggy marshland areas where bright green *Sphagnum* moss grows. Listen for its song and try to spot one. *Never* venture onto the bog itself.

▼ Mottled grasshopper
This common heathland species has mottled colouring varying from green to brown.

Potter wasp ▲
Little flask-shaped nests among heather, stocked with paralysed insects, belong to potter wasps.

▼ Emperor moth
Found on heaths and moors, day-flying emperor moths are very active. The caterpillars are camouflaged among heather.

▲ Green tiger beetle
This is a fierce and active predator, often seen along heathland paths.

FRESH WATER

In spring, most aquatic plants have not begun to grow and so observation of pond animals is relatively easy. In late spring, adult dragonflies emerge from the nymphs. Dragonflies, like many other insects, often emerge at night. In the morning, recently emerged insects sit on the waterside vegetation. Midday is a good time to watch for water beetles and bugs, which are most easily seen in the summer months.

Dragonfly ▼
Adult dragonflies sometimes remain near their cast skin until morning, so search for them at dawn.

▼ Whirlygig beetle
Large numbers of whirlygigs are a common sight on a pool surface. When disturbed, they dive deep, but they soon return.

Dragonfly hatching ▲
In spring, larvae leave the water and climb up vegetation prior to emergence as adults.

Water scorpion ▶
The water scorpion remains motionless and camouflaged while waiting for prey. It has a long breathing tube which breaks the water surface.

▼ Damselfly
Adult damselflies and dragonflies catch insects on the wing.

PROJECT

Pond-dipping is great fun. Approach the water quietly. First, pass your net along the surface of the water to gather surface specimens. Next, swish the net through the weeds, Lastly, check out the bottom. Put your specimens in pond water in small containers, and use a hand lens to examine them closely. Do not forget to pour everything back.

▼ Water boatman
Hanging from the underside of the surface film, water boatmen feed on other insects. They look silvery because of trapped air bubbles.

◄ Mosquito larva
Mosquito and midge larvae live at the surface of still, stagnant ponds.

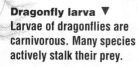

Diving beetle ▼
The diving beetle is an active swimmer and fierce predator. Its air supply is held under its wing cases.

Dragonfly larva ▼
Larvae of dragonflies are carnivorous. Many species actively stalk their prey.

THE URBAN ENVIRONMENT

The urban environment is important for wildlife because man-made habitats provide shelter and sanctuary for a wide range of insects. Some live inside our houses and buildings, while others like the garden soil or the plants that we grow. Garden ponds are also important for freshwater insects. Butterflies are frequent visitors to our garden flowers by day, while moths are attracted at night. Wasps make their nests in our houses and feed on rotting fruit. Lacewings and oak bush crickets live in the garden.

Lacewing ▼
Both adults and larvae eat aphids and other insects, so their presence in the garden is beneficial. In the autumn, they may come indoors to hibernate. They are attracted to lights at night.

▲ Small tortoiseshell
Small tortoiseshells are extremely fond of buddleia, ice-plant and many other garden flowers.

◄ Peacock butterfly
Also attracted to garden flowers, this butterfly may hibernate indoors during the winter months. It may 'wake up' on warm days.

House fly ►
Ever-present around houses during the summer months, house flies feed on liquid food and lay their eggs on putrefying meat.

Ladybird ▲
Ladybirds are gardeners' friends. They destroy hundreds of pests such as aphids, which attack roses, broad beans and other garden plants.

◄ Cockroach
Many hotels and large kitchens have cockroaches. They are mainly nocturnal and come out to feed on scraps of food.

If you would like to attract more butterflies to your garden, try growing species of flowers that they like. Buddleia, ice-plant and Michaelmas Daisy are particular favourites and should be planted in a sunny border. Keep a record of how many species you see. If you would like to encourage some to breed, leave a 'wild' patch with nettles and thistles. Small tortoiseshells and peacocks (right) may lay eggs there.

Wasps ▼
Wasps are fond of fruit and are especially attracted to rotting apples.

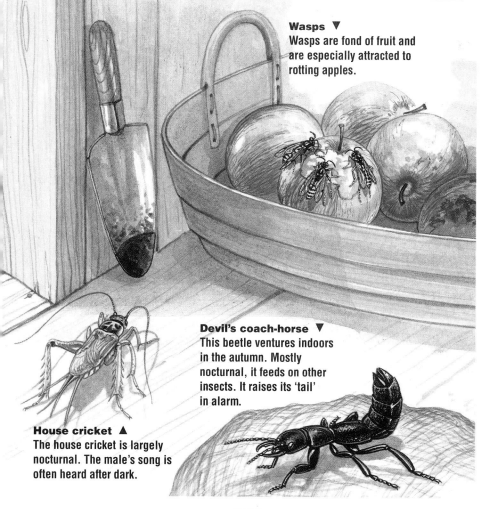

Devil's coach-horse ▼
This beetle ventures indoors in the autumn. Mostly nocturnal, it feeds on other insects. It raises its 'tail' in alarm.

House cricket ▲
The house cricket is largely nocturnal. The male's song is often heard after dark.

MAYFLIES AND PRIMITIVES

CHARACTERISTICS

Mayflies are common freshwater insects, with two pairs of unequal wings. The nymphs live in clean water. They have gills along their abdomens and three bristle-like 'tails' at the tip. Stoneflies look flattened and have wings held folded over the body at rest. The nymphs have two bristles at the end of the abdomen. Springtails and silverfish are primitive insects which lack wings.

HABITS

Adult mayflies usually live a day or so, and occur in large swarms. Stoneflies live for a few weeks. They often crawl over waterside stones and vegetation, and fly weakly.

Mayflies are unusual insects: the first stage in the life cycle which has wings is not the adult. Instead, it is called the sub-imago. Shortly after it hatches from the nymph, the sub-imago moults to become a full adult. The adult can fly straight away.

MAYFLY
Ephemera danica
L 17mm. Large, with well-marked wings. Common in slow rivers and lakes.

Visit a river bank in May or June on a warm, still evening and you may well see a mayfly swarm. The males form large swarms which dance over the water's surface. If a female strays into the swarm, she is grabbed by the male and mating occurs on the wing. The eggs are laid – some species just drop them on the water – and in many species the adults die afterwards.

SPRINGTAIL ▽
Podura aquatica
L 3mm. Common on the surface of ponds. Leaps when disturbed.

STONEFLY ▲
Chloroperla torrentium
L 7mm. Very common in fast-flowing stony streams. Found among bankside vegetation.

MAYFLY ▽
Chloeon dipterum
L 5mm. Common in slow-moving and still water. Rather weak flight.

SILVERFISH ▲
Lepisma saccharina
L 11mm. Often found in cupboards. Shuns daylight; seen mostly after dark.

DRAGONFLIES

BROAD-BODIED LIBELLULA
Libellula depressa
L 40mm. Shallow lakes and
ponds. Common in summer.

CHARACTERISTICS

Dragonflies are impressive insects with two
pairs of powerful clear wings which enable
them to catch insects on the wing. They have
large eyes for spotting their prey.

HABITS

Dragonfly nymphs live in water and so the
adults are usually seen near ponds, rivers and
lakes. Some species have a feeding territory
which they guard from other dragonflies – their
clattering wings can be heard as they battle.
When they mate, most species fly around in
tandem before they lay their eggs in the water
or among the waterside vegetation. The
nymphs, too, are active predators: some species
tackle prey as large as tadpoles or small fish.

A dragonfly's eyes are large
and give it almost all-round
vision. They are sensitive to
the slightest movement
around them. If you look
closely you will be able to
see the individual facets of
the eye. Each one contains
its own lens; together they
help form the image seen.

EMPEROR DRAGONFLY
Anax imperator
L 77mm. Body greenish before mature. Common near lakes.

♂

♀

♀

♂

COMMON DARTER
Sympetrum striolatum
L 35mm. Body paler before mature. Common until autumn.

♀

♂

♂

♀

CLUB-TAILED DRAGONFLY
Gomphus vulgatissimus
L 40mm. Slow-moving rivers. Local and southern.

GOLDEN-RINGED DRAGONFLY
Cordulegaster boltonii
L 70mm. Found near streams on moors and heaths. Common.

♂

♀

♀

♂

BROWN HAWKER
Aeshna grandis
L 65mm. Brownish wings and blue eyes. Common near ponds.

KEELED SKIMMER
Orthetrum coerulescens
L 40mm. Active and alert. Boggy pools and ponds. Common.

DAMSELFLIES

CHARACTERISTICS

These delicate insects belong to the sub-order Zygoptera, a sub division of the order Odonata. They have forewings and hindwings roughly similar in size and shape. These are transparent and membranous and criss-crossed with veins. Most have the wings folded above the body.

Unlike the closely positioned eyes of dragonflies, damselfly eyes are always widely separated, projecting at the side of the head.

HABITS

Damselflies are rather weak fliers. The larvae are aquatic. They have long, slender bodies with three projections at the abdomen for breathing dissolved oxygen.

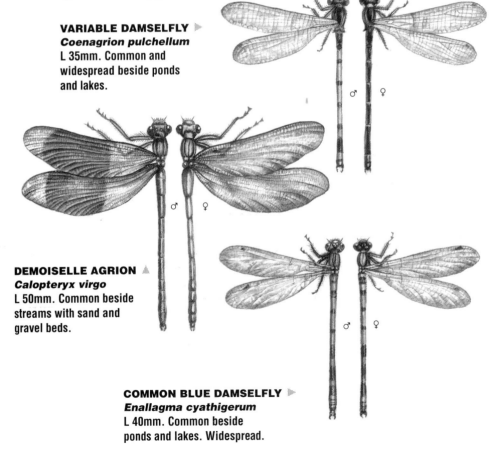

VARIABLE DAMSELFLY ▷
Coenagrion pulchellum
L 35mm. Common and widespread beside ponds and lakes.

DEMOISELLE AGRION ▲
Calopteryx virgo
L 50mm. Common beside streams with sand and gravel beds.

COMMON BLUE DAMSELFLY ▷
Enallagma cyathigerum
L 40mm. Common beside ponds and lakes. Widespread.

PROJECT

In the late spring or summer, the damselfly larva leaves the water. It secures itself about a metre from the surface and then emerges as an adult. This transformation is one of the most remarkable events in nature. Carefully collect the cast skin – called an *exuvia* – in a collecting pot after the damselfly has flown away. Be careful because it is extremely delicate and easily damaged. The species of damselfly can be identified from this exact replica of the damselfly's final larval stage.

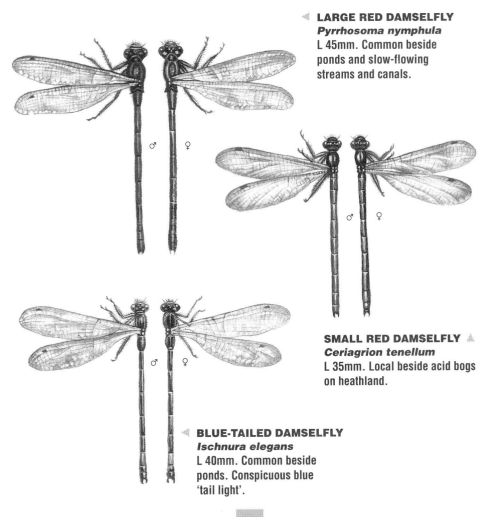

LARGE RED DAMSELFLY
Pyrrhosoma nymphula
L 45mm. Common beside ponds and slow-flowing streams and canals.

SMALL RED DAMSELFLY
Ceriagrion tenellum
L 35mm. Local beside acid bogs on heathland.

BLUE-TAILED DAMSELFLY
Ischnura elegans
L 40mm. Common beside ponds. Conspicuous blue 'tail light'.

GRASSHOPPERS

CHARACTERISTICS

Grasshoppers are members of a group of insects called Orthoptera. Literally, this means 'straight-wings'. They have powerful hind legs with which they can hop to escape danger. Some species have wings and can fly for short distances. Males are usually smaller than females of the same species.

Grasshoppers sing using their wings and legs, not with their mouths. The hind legs have a row of pegs on their inner surface. When the legs are moved up and down, the pegs rub against a rough surface on the wing. This produces the characteristic, rasping song.

HABITS

During sunny weather, male grasshoppers 'sing' to attract females. Most grasshoppers live in grassy places but a few live on heathlands and bogs. Mole-crickets and groundhoppers are related to grasshoppers. Mole-crickets have powerful front legs and burrow in soil. Groundhoppers are small creatures which hop well and are easily overlooked.

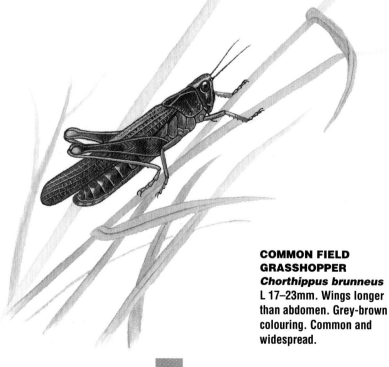

COMMON FIELD GRASSHOPPER
Chorthippus brunneus
L 17–23mm. Wings longer than abdomen. Grey-brown colouring. Common and widespread.

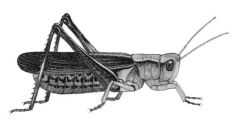

LARGE MARSH GRASSHOPPER
Stethophyma grossum
L 27–33mm. Lives on heathland bogs. Flies actively.

MEADOW GRASSHOPPER
Chorthippus parallelus
L 13–20mm. Females have very short wings, males slightly longer. Several colour forms.

STRIPE-WINGED GRASSHOPPER
Stenobothrus lineatus
L 17–20mm. Found on chalk grassland. White wing stripe and blotch.

COMMON GREEN GRASSHOPPER
Omocestus viridulus
L 16–20mm. A common grassland species. Invariably green in colour.

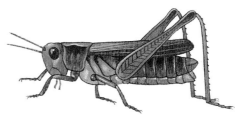

MOTTLED GRASSHOPPER
Myrmeleotettix maculatus
L 13–16mm. A small species with club-tipped antennae. Beautifully mottled markings.

MOLE-CRICKET
Gryllotalpa gryllotalpa
L 40mm. Lives underground but may emerge at night. Covered in velvety hairs.

COMMON GROUNDHOPPER
Tetrix undulata
L 6mm. Extremely active. Found in spring and autumn.

BUSH CRICKETS

CHARACTERISTICS

Bush crickets are related to grasshoppers but they have antennae which are longer than the body. Female bush crickets have a long, pointed ovipositor which is used to lay eggs.

HABITS

Some species place their eggs in the soil, while others insert them into plant stems. Bush crickets have long, slender legs with which they climb through vegetation. The hind legs, in particular, are especially elongated and enable them to hop powerfully. Males sing but some songs are inaudible to the human ear. True crickets are related to bush crickets. They scuttle when danger approaches.

Unlike grasshoppers, bush crickets 'sing' by rubbing their wings together. A row of pegs on one wing rubs against a rough surface on the other, producing a rasping sound.

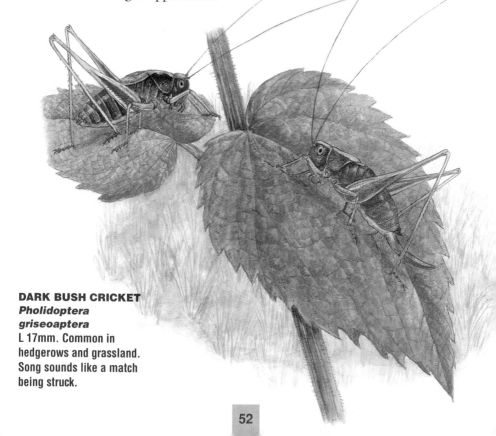

DARK BUSH CRICKET
Pholidoptera
griseoaptera
L 17mm. Common in hedgerows and grassland. Song sounds like a match being struck.

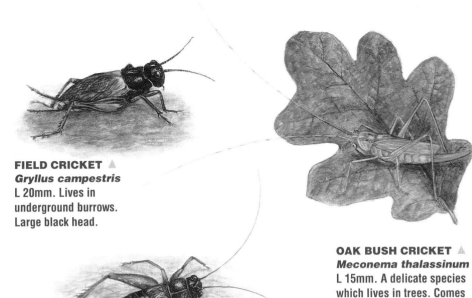

FIELD CRICKET ▲
Gryllus campestris
L 20mm. Lives in
underground burrows.
Large black head.

OAK BUSH CRICKET ▲
Meconema thalassinum
L 15mm. A delicate species
which lives in trees. Comes
to house lights at night.

WOOD CRICKET ▲
Nemobius sylvestris
L 10mm. Lives in colonies in
leaf litter, especially beech.

▼ **BOG BUSH CRICKET**
Leptophyes punctatissima
L 10mm. Common on
brambles. Female has
scythe-shaped ovipositor.

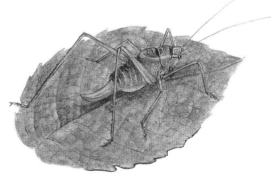

SPECKLED BUSH CRICKET ▲
Metrioptera brachyptera
L 16mm. Found on damp
heathland. Very active.

MANTIDS AND COCKROACHES

CHARACTERISTICS

Praying mantids and cockroaches are related to each other. Mantids have a narrow thorax and triangular-shaped head with powerful mouthparts. Cockroaches are flattened insects with long antennae. Earwigs have semi-circular hindwings which are kept folded. They are distinguished by the pincer-like cerci at the end of the abdomen.

HABITS

Mantids are carnivorous. The struggling prey is held in the front legs. Cockroaches feed on organic debris and are often associated with man. Earwigs are generally nocturnal and feed on anything from plant matter to small insects. Stick insects eat leaves; their shape provides good camouflage among twigs and branches.

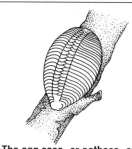

The egg case, or ootheca, of a praying mantid is spongy at first but becomes extremely hard. It is attached to twigs and stems by the female. The young mantids easily escape from this when they hatch. At first they are worm-like but they soon resemble miniature adults.

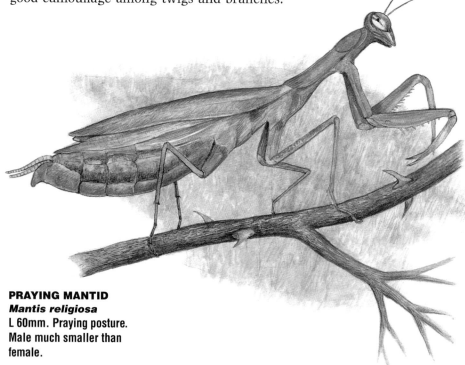

PRAYING MANTID
Mantis religiosa
L 60mm. Praying posture.
Male much smaller than
female.

PRAYING MANTID ▽
Iris oratoria
L 35mm. Eye spot on
hindwing. Shortish wings.

STICK INSECT ▽
Bacillus rossii
L 70mm. Slender, green body
and legs. Lacks wings.
Antennae are short.

◁ TAWNY COCKROACH
Ectobius pallidus
L 7mm. Found in grassland
and woods. Flies readily.
Common and widespread
but overlooked.

AMERICAN COCKROACH ▷
Periplaneta americana
L 30mm. Golden-brown and
shiny. Lives in buildings.
Common.

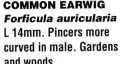

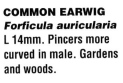

◁ COMMON EARWIG
Forficula auricularia
L 14mm. Pincers more
curved in male. Gardens
and woods.

WATER BUGS

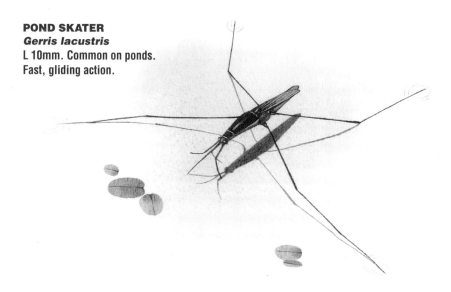

POND SKATER
Gerris lacustris
L 10mm. Common on ponds.
Fast, gliding action.

CHARACTERISTICS

Freshwater ponds and lakes hold many species of water bugs. Like their land-based relatives, they have piercing mouthparts. Most species are carnivorous and attack living prey.

HABITS

Pond skaters and water-measurers live on the surface of the water. Their legs spread the weight of their bodies so that they do not break the surface film. Those water bugs that live in the water still breathe air. Water scorpions and water stick insects move slowly, relying on camouflage to avoid detection. Water boatmen are strong swimmers. Paddle-shaped legs, which are fringed with hairs, help them to move easily through the water.

The pond skater is very sensitive to movements in the surface film of the pond. If a fly or beetle becomes trapped and struggles, it attracts the skater. This then pierces it with its pointed mouthparts. Pond skaters seem to glide effortlessly over the water's surface.

WATER SCORPION
Nepa cinerea
L 25mm. Flattened, leaf-like body. Pincer-like front legs and pointed mouthparts.

WATER BOATMAN ▶
Notonecta glauca
L 10mm. Swims upside down. Can fly well, away from water.

WATER-MEASURER ▲
Hydrometra stagnorum
L 9mm. Lives on the surface but catches submerged prey.

PROJECT

See how water bugs breathe. They all need air, and in order to breathe, water stick insects (below) and water scorpions have breathing tubes. The water boatman and lesser water boatman carry air trapped in their body surface. This gives them a silvery appearance as they swim. Although they can stay underwater for quite long periods, they have to return to the surface from time to time to get a fresh supply of air.

WATER STICK INSECT
Ranatra linearis
L 45mm. Stick-like and slow-moving. Pincer-like front legs grab and hold prey.

LESSER WATER BOATMAN ▼
Corixa punctata
L 10mm. Swims the right way up. Hind legs are fringed with hairs.

SHIELDBUGS

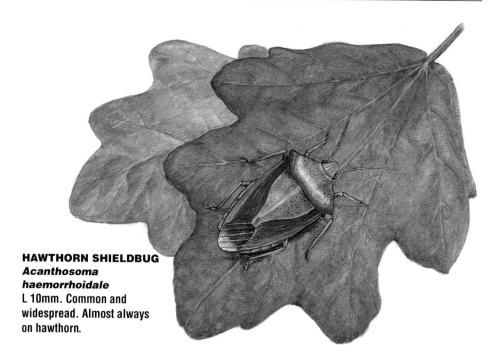

HAWTHORN SHIELDBUG
*Acanthosoma
haemorrhoidale*
L 10mm. Common and
widespread. Almost always
on hawthorn.

CHARACTERISTICS

The body of a shieldbug is rather flattened and
is roughly triangular. The shield-shaped
appearance earns them their name. They are
rather slow-moving and have powerful,
piercing mouthparts.

HABITS

Some shieldbugs suck plant sap and the juice of
berries, while others attack other insects such
as caterpillars. Many species live in trees or
bushes and they can be caught in a beating
tray. Some species are found only in one type
of tree or bush. The parent bug is particularly
unusual: it guards its eggs and young until
they can fend for themselves. This saves them
from being attacked by parasitic wasps or eaten
by other insects. Some shieldbugs hibernate.

Some shieldbugs cause
damage to fruit crops. For
example, the raspberry
shieldbug attacks the ripe
fruit and sucks the juices.
This not only damages the
raspberry directly but it also
allows other organisms, such
as fungi, to attack it.

Search hedgerow vegetation to study shieldbugs feeding. Some species of shieldbug are not content to feed on plant sap, berries and fruit. Soft-bodied insects, especially if they cannot defend themselves, are a good meal. Caterpillars are vulnerable to attack and, once pierced, have little hope of escaping alive.

PARENT BUG
Elasmucha grisea
L 9mm. Found in birchwoods. Females guard their eggs and young.

GORSE SHIELDBUG
Piezodorus lituratus
L 7mm. Found on sprays of gorse on heathlands. Colour matches that of gorse leaves.

Graphosoma italicum
L 10mm. Found on flower heads, especially umbellifers. Not found in Britain but common in mainland Europe.

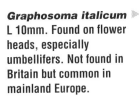

GREEN SHIELDBUG
Palomena prasina
L 8mm. Common and widespread. Found in bushes. Well camouflaged.

FOREST BUG
Pentatoma rufipes
L 11mm. Common in woodland, often in oak trees. Will attack other insects.

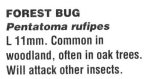

OTHER BUGS

CHARACTERISTICS

Like shieldbugs, the bugs illustrated here belong to the order Hemiptera. All have sharp, pointed mouthparts for sucking plant or animal juices.

HABITS AND HABITAT

Many species of bug can be found by using a sweep net in grassland or with a beating tray among bushes. They often have rather soft bodies and so must be handled with care. One group of bugs, called capsid bugs, contains several species which cause damage to fruit and other crops. Some species are predatory and may help control other pests. One species of bug, the bed bug, was formerly very common, until improved living standards made it comparatively rare.

When bugs mate, they may remain joined together at the tips of the abdomens for some time. This ensures that fertilisation is successful. After mating has taken place, the male and female part and go their separate ways. The female then lays the eggs in a suitable, safe site.

FIREBUG
Pyrrhocoris apterus
L 9mm. May form large swarms on tree trunks or on ground. Rare and local in Britain.

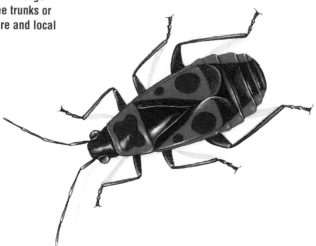

Assassin bugs are well named. They attack other insects and suck their body fluids. Caterpillars are a favourite food because they have soft bodies and often no means of defence. If you visit a heathland during the summer and search the heather you may find a heath assassin bug attacking its prey. They are often found among the sprays of flowers.

BLACK-KNEED BUG
Blepharidopterus angulatus
L 6mm. Often found on fruit trees. Eats red spider mites.

BED BUG
Cimex lectularius
L 5mm. Hides during daytime. Sucks blood after dark.

MARSH DAMSEL BUG
Dolichonabis limbatus
L 10mm. Common in marsh fields, attacking other insects.

HEATH ASSASSIN BUG
Coranus subapterus
L 10mm. Found on sandy heaths. Occasionally fully winged.

GREEN CAPSID BUG
Lygocoris pabulinus
L 5mm. Common on plants. May attack fruit and vegetables.

APHIDS AND THEIR ALLIES

CHARACTERISTICS

Aphids and their allies are related to bugs but are classified in a different group. Aphids are tiny insects that feed on plant sap and are usually wingless. Cicadas and leafhoppers hold their wings over the body when at rest.

HABITS

Aphids are often found in large colonies and are usually wingless. At certain times of the year, some species produce winged forms which disperse to new areas. Some aphids cause considerable damage to crops and in gardens. Cicadas make a loud, high-pitched song. The further south in Europe you travel, the more common they become. Leafhoppers feed on plant sap and can hop well.

Nature has its own way of controlling aphid populations if they build up to large numbers. The populations of ladybirds, and other aphid predators, soon build up too. Both adult and larval ladybirds eat the aphids. One individual may consume hundreds during its lifetime.

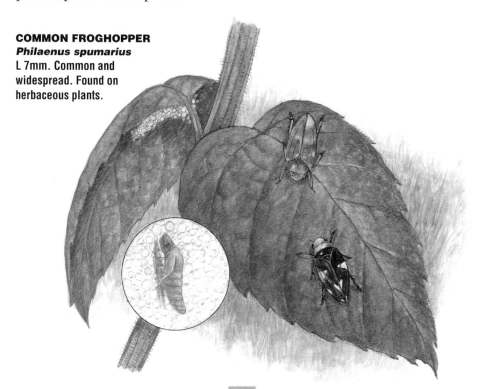

COMMON FROGHOPPER
Philaenus spumarius
L 7mm. Common and widespread. Found on herbaceous plants.

RED AND BLACK LEAFHOPPER ▼
Cercopis vulnerata
L 11mm. Common in woods
and hedgerows. Hops when it
is disturbed.

CICADA ▲
Tibicen plebejus
L 35mm. Difficult to locate.
Newly emerged adults
sometimes found in morning.

ROSE APHID ▲
Macrosiphium rosae
L 2mm. Common on roses.
The common 'greenfly'.

CABBAGE APHID ▲
Brevicoryne brassicae
L 2mm. Common on
cabbages and related plants.
Mostly wingless forms.

◀ **BLACK BEAN APHID**
Aphis fabae
L 2mm. The gardener's
'blackfly'. Common.

WOOLLY APHID ▲
Eriosoma lanigerum
L 2mm. Body covered in
woolly hairs. Lives in dense
clusters on apple and several
other trees.

SCORPION FLIES AND LACEWINGS

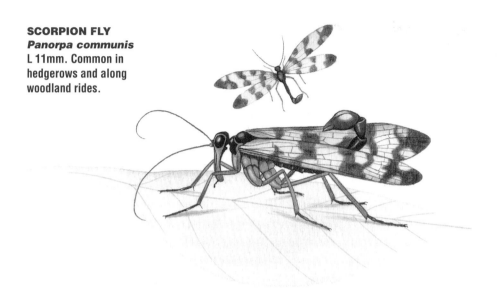

SCORPION FLY
Panorpa communis
L 11mm. Common in
hedgerows and along
woodland rides.

CHARACTERISTICS

Lacewings, alder flies, ant-lions and butterfly lions belong to the order Neuroptera, which literally means 'nerve-winged' – the wings are covered in a fine network of veins. Although the wings are obviously well developed, most species fly quite weakly.

HABITS

The larvae of lacewings are free-living and carnivorous. They eat aphids and can be difficult to spot since they cover themselves in the dead remains of their prey. Ant-lion larvae are also carnivorous. They live in sandy soil and dig little pits into which ants, and other small insects, fall and are caught. The scorpion fly's English name comes from the shape of the tip of the abdomen in the male. They fly short distances and hide if alarmed.

Scorpion flies seem able to walk across a spider's web as easily as the spider itself. Since many spiders wrap their victims but do not eat them immediately there are free meals for alert scorpion flies. The long beak-shaped mouthparts are suited to scavenging for meals.

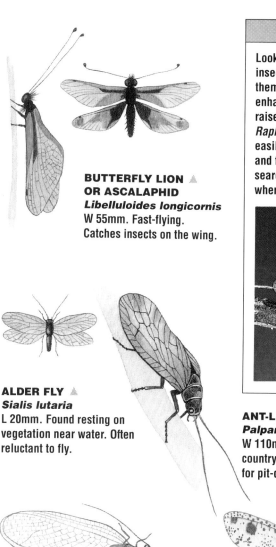

BUTTERFLY LION ▲
OR ASCALAPHID
Libelluloides longicornis
W 55mm. Fast-flying.
Catches insects on the wing.

PROJECT

Look for snake flies, which are curious insects with a long 'neck'. This gives them a snake-like appearance which is enhanced when the neck and head are raised like a cobra. One species, *Raphida notata*, is widespread but easily disturbed. It lives in oak woods and feeds mainly on aphids. To find it, search among the leaves, especially where there are aphids.

ALDER FLY ▲
Sialis lutaria
L 20mm. Found resting on vegetation near water. Often reluctant to fly.

ANT-LION ▼
Palpares libelluloides
W 110mm. Found in open country where soil suitable for pit-dwelling larvae.

◀ **GREEN LACEWING**
Chrysops carnea
L 18mm. Found in bushes and trees. Comes indoors in the autumn.

BUTTERFLIES

Swallowtail eggs are laid on fennel, milk parsley and other plants in the umbellifer family. The caterpillars are brightly marked to warn predators of their unpleasant taste. The pupae are attached to the stem of the foodplant by the tip of the abdomen and a silk 'girdle'.

SWALLOWTAIL
Papilio machaon
W 80mm. A conspicuous and active species.

CHARACTERISTICS

Swallowtails and apollos belong to the same family. They have brightly marked caterpillars. The 'whites' belong to a different family, with slender bodies and white wings.

HABITS AND DISTRIBUTION

Swallowtails fly near wet ditches and marshes where they feed on nectar. In Britain they are confined to parts of East Anglia, but in mainland Europe they are common and widespread. The apollo is confined to mountainous regions, whereas all three species of white are widespread.

In hot weather, butterflies need to drink a lot. They can be seen congregating around drying pools. They also take in important salts.

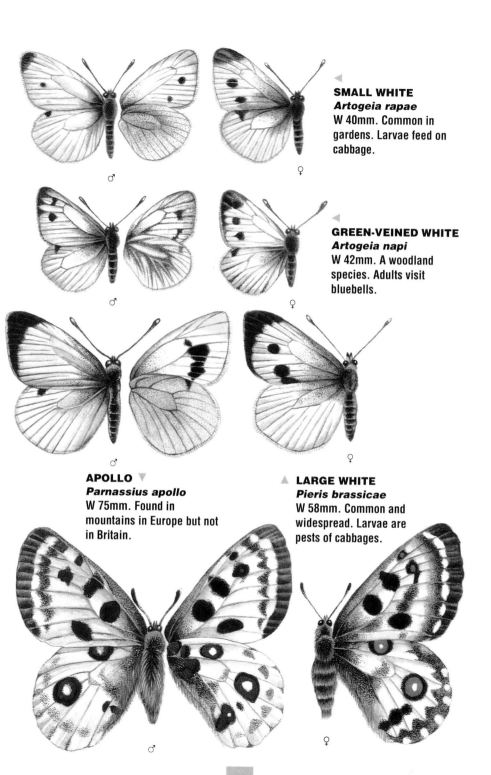

SMALL WHITE
Artogeia rapae
W 40mm. Common in
gardens. Larvae feed on
cabbage.

♂   ♀

GREEN-VEINED WHITE
Artogeia napi
W 42mm. A woodland
species. Adults visit
bluebells.

♂   ♀

♂   ♀

APOLLO
Parnassius apollo
W 75mm. Found in
mountains in Europe but not
in Britain.

LARGE WHITE
Pieris brassicae
W 58mm. Common and
widespread. Larvae are
pests of cabbages.

♂   ♀

BUTTERFLIES

CHARACTERISTICS

These white and yellow butterflies belong to the same family as the 'whites'. Female brimstones may be mistaken for large whites in flight. Bath whites and female orange tips superficially resemble green-veined whites.

HABITS

Brimstones hatch from the pupae in autumn and hibernate during the winter emerging as early as March or April. They are often found along woodland rides. The other species are found in woods and meadows.

Most butterflies, including the brimstone, visit flowers to feed. They use their long proboscis to reach nectar.

The female brimstone lays her eggs on the underside of the leaves of buckthorn and alder buckthorn. The caterpillar often rests along the midrib of the leaf. The chrysalis looks like a curled-up leaf. It is attached with a silk thread around its body.

BRIMSTONE
Gonepteryx rhamni
W 50mm. Common and widespread, spring and autumn.

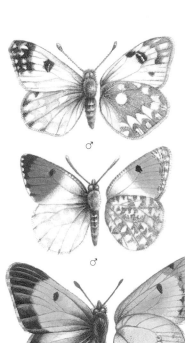

BATH WHITE
Pontia daplidice
W 45mm. Active flier. Rare
visitor to Britain.

♂ ♀

ORANGE TIP
Anthocharis cardamines
W 40mm. Woodland rides
and paths. Common in
spring.

♂ ♀

CLOUDED YELLOW
Colias croceus
W 55mm. Annual migrant to
Britain from Europe.

♂ ♀

♀

WOOD WHITE ▲
Leptidea sinapis
W 35mm. Delicate flight.
A local woodland species.

BLACK-VEINED WHITE ▲ ♂
Aporia crataegi
W 50mm. Extinct in Britain
but common in Europe.
Hedgerows.

PROJECT

Look for orange tips, which are
extremely active butterflies. Their
emergence in the spring coincides with
the appearance of woodland flowers
such as bluebells and primroses. They
feed on the nectar; and this is the best
time to try to photograph them.

BUTTERFLIES

CHARACTERISTICS AND DISTRIBUTION

The butterflies illustrated all belong to the same family. The upperwing colouring is very different from that on the underwings. Most are rather local woodland species, although the small tortoiseshell is widespread.

HABITS

The purple emperor is a 'blue-riband' species for the butterfly watchers in Britain. It occurs only in the south. It is often seen flying around the tree tops, although it does descend to feed on the ground. The other species feed on flowers along woodland rides.

Purple emperors are well known for visiting dung. They drink the moisture and salts with their long tongues.

♂

♀

The female purple emperor lays her eggs on sallow leaves. In the summer these hatch into small larvae, which hibernate until the next spring. The chrysalis looks like a sallow leaf.

PURPLE EMPEROR
Apatura iris
W 65mm. Local and rather scarce in woodlands.

LARGE TORTOISESHELL
Nymphalis polychloros
W 60mm. Very rare in
Britain. Widespread in
Europe.

WHITE ADMIRAL
Limenitis camilla
W 50mm. Visits bramble
flowers, especially along
woodland rides.

SMALL TORTOISESHELL
Aglais urticae
W 45mm. Common in
gardens and fields. Larvae
feed on nettles.

COMMA
Polygonia c-album
W 45mm. Two generations
per year. Visits brambles.

MAP BUTTERFLY
Araschnia levana
W 35mm. A woodland
species. Larvae feed on
nettles. Not in Britain.

BUTTERFLIES

CHARACTERISTICS

All the species illustrated are alert and active fliers, and belong to the same family.

HABITS

Peacocks and red admirals like garden flowers. They also feed on rotting fruit in the autumn. Peacocks hibernate, sometimes waking on mild winter days. The Camberwell beauty hibernates in hollow trees. Dark green and high brown fritillaries are fond of thistles and knapweeds, and are difficult to approach.

The eye spots on the upper wing of the peacock are extremely life-like. They startle potential predators when the wings are suddenly flashed open.

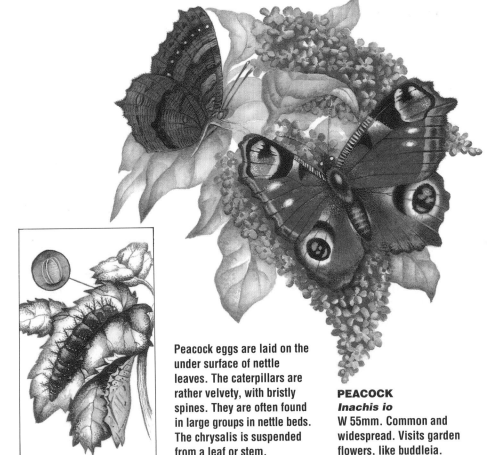

Peacock eggs are laid on the under surface of nettle leaves. The caterpillars are rather velvety, with bristly spines. They are often found in large groups in nettle beds. The chrysalis is suspended from a leaf or stem.

PEACOCK
Inachis io
W 55mm. Common and widespread. Visits garden flowers, like buddleia.

CAMBERWELL BEAUTY
Nymphalis antiopa
W 60mm. Rare visitor to
Britain. Widespread in
Europe.

PAINTED LADY ▼
Cynthia cardui
W 55mm. A migrant species.
Caterpillars on thistles.

RED ADMIRAL ▲
Vanessa atalanta
W 60mm. Migrant to northern
Europe. Widespread.

PROJECT

Look for dark green fritillaries, which
are often found on chalk grassland. One
of the most conspicuous flowers of this
habitat is the greater knapweed. The
fritillaries love to feed on its nectar, and
sometimes two or three individuals
congregate on a single flower. Dark
green fritillaries are normally difficult
to photograph. However, if you set your
camera up, pointing on a flower of
greater knapweed, the butterflies may
come to feed on it.

HIGH BROWN FRITILLARY ▼
Fabriciana adippe
W 50mm. A local species.
Grassy places throughout.

DARK GREEN FRITILLARY ▼
Mesoacidalia aglaja
W 55mm. Grassy places,
often on chalk. Very active.

BUTTERFLIES

CHARACTERISTICS

Fritillaries have orange-brown upperwings with black spots. The underwings are beautifully marked. The Duke of Burgundy fritillary is *not* related to other fritillaries, but belongs to a group of butterflies known as 'metalmarks'.

HABITS AND HABITAT

Pearl-bordered fritillaries are found only where the light conditions allow a good growth of violets – the larval foodplants. The small pearl-bordered fritillary is rather similar and is on the wing in June and July. The black markings on the underwing are rather darker in this species than in the pearl-bordered fritillary. It also occurs along woodland rides.

Fritillaries are renowned sun-loving insects. In dull weather they are completely inactive. In the mornings and late afternoons they often sunbathe to warm their bodies.

♀

The eggs of pearl-bordered fritillaries are laid on the leaves of dog violet. After feeding in the summer, the caterpillars hibernate. They emerge in spring to feed.

♂

PEARL-BORDERED FRITILLARY
Boloria euphrosyne
W 45mm. Locally common along woodland rides.

SILVER-WASHED FRITILLARY
Argynnis paphia
W 60mm. Woodland rides. Often feeds on bramble flowers.

HEATH FRITILLARY ▲
Mellicta athalia
W 35mm. Local in Britain. Larvae feed on cow-wheat.

QUEEN OF SPAIN FRITILLARY ▲
Issoria lathonia
W 50mm. A renowned migrant. Rare visitor to Britain.

PROJECT

Marsh fritillaries are active only in warm weather. As soon as the sun disappears, they stop flying and hide in the vegetation. Early morning and late afternoon are good times to see them sunbathing – catching the warmth of the sun's rays. They can then often be approached closely and photographed. On dull days, they will sometimes even crawl on to your finger.

DUKE OF BURGUNDY FRITILLARY ▲
Hamearis lucina
W 27mm. Local on chalk downs. Larvae feed on cowslips.

MARSH FRITILLARY ▲
Eurodryas aurinia
W 40mm. Local in wet meadows. Larvae on scabious.

BUTTERFLIES

CHARACTERISTICS

The browns – family Satyridae – are a diverse group of butterflies which are generally associated with grassland. Their larvae feed on grass leaves.

HABITS AND HABITATS

In Britain, the Scotch argus is confined to the north, preferring upland meadows but sometimes occurring in open, pine woodland. It is widespread in Europe. In overcast weather this butterfly sits among grasses, while in bright sunshine it flies actively.

The caterpillars of most species of brown butterfly feed at night on grasses. Take a torch and inspect the grasses in a meadow after dark to find them.

The eggs of the Scotch argus are laid on the leaves of grasses, especially purple moor grass. The larvae hibernate, and emerge to feed in spring. The chrysalis is formed at the base of clumps of grasses.

SCOTCH ARGUS
Erebia aethiops
W 45mm. An upland species. Locally common.

MARBLED WHITE
Melanargia galathea
W 45mm. Locally common in grassy meadows.

GRAYLING
Hipparchia semele
W 45mm. Heaths and bare grassy patches. Local.

RINGLET
Aphantopus hyperantus
W 42mm. Meadows and woodland rides. Common throughout Europe.

GATEKEEPER
Pyronia tithonus
W 40mm. Hedges, bramble patches and woodland rides.

MEADOW BROWN
Maniola jurtina
W 45mm. Meadows and hedges. Often visits bramble flowers.

BUTTERFLIES

PURPLE HAIRSTREAK
Quercusia quercus
W 35mm. Locally common in oak woodland.

The female purple hairstreak lays her eggs singly on the twigs of oak. The larva is flattened and difficult to spot. The pupa is attached to bark or leaves.

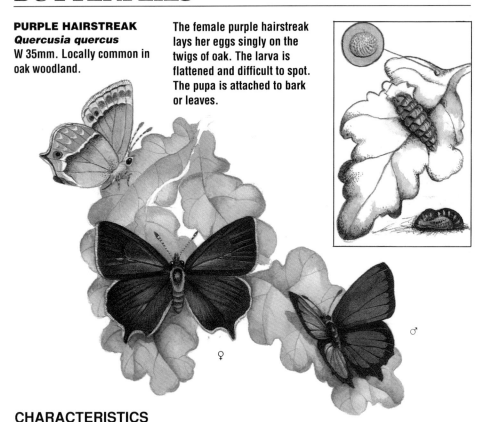

♀

♂

CHARACTERISTICS

Hairstreaks belong to the 'blue' family and have small, tail-like projections on the hind-wings. The larvae are grub-like. The others belong to the 'brown' family. Their larvae feed on grasses and spend the winter as caterpillars.

HABITS

Purple and white-letter hairstreaks fly around tree tops, large groups congregating around favoured spots. Their pale underwings can make them rather difficult to spot flying against the sky. The speckled wood favours sunny woodland rides. The wall brown likes dry, sunny spots, such as rocks and walls, while the small heath is a meadow species.

Purple hairstreaks can often be seen feeding on honeydew – a sugary fluid produced by aphids – on the surface of oak leaves. To find it, they walk slowly across the leaf surface, probing with their proboscis.

WALL BROWN ▷
Lasiommata megera
W 45mm. Rather local in dry,
grassy places.
Sunbathes.

♂   ♀

♂   ♀   ♂

SPECKLED WOOD ▲
Pararge aegeria
W 45mm. Woodland rides.
Males fight. Often sunbathes.

WHITE-LETTER HAIRSTREAK ▲
Strymonidia w-album
W 32mm. Colonies often on
single elm trees. Local.

PROJECT

Watch speckled woods fight. The male
speckled wood guards its own sunny
glade or clearing in a woodland. If
another male intrudes into this territory,
the owner drives him away by engaging
in spiralling aerial battles. Neither
male gets damaged during these
aggressive-looking encounters.

♂

GREEN HAIRSTREAK ▲
Callophrys rubi
W 25mm. Well camouflaged
at rest. Locally common.

♂   ♀

SMALL HEATH ▲
Coenonympha pamphilus
W 30mm. Common in
grassland. Hides in dull weather.

BUTTERFLIES

CHARACTERISTICS

'Blues' belong to a huge family of small butterflies called the Lycaenidae. Most males have blue upperwings, though some females and a few males are brown. Study the black, orange and white spots on the underwings and see how each species is different.

HABITS

Blue butterflies like to sunbathe and are most easily approached early in the morning as they bask in the sun's rays. On hot days, they may visit puddles to drink. Their caterpillars are shaped like woodlice.

A pair of small blues mating: they are joined at the tips of their abdomens. They may remain together for over an hour before parting.

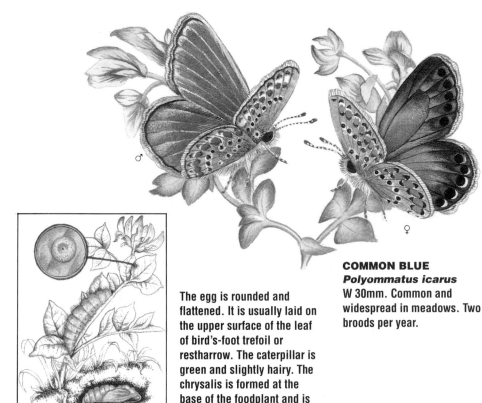

♂

♀

The egg is rounded and flattened. It is usually laid on the upper surface of the leaf of bird's-foot trefoil or restharrow. The caterpillar is green and slightly hairy. The chrysalis is formed at the base of the foodplant and is buried by ants.

COMMON BLUE
Polyommatus icarus
W 30mm. Common and widespread in meadows. Two broods per year.

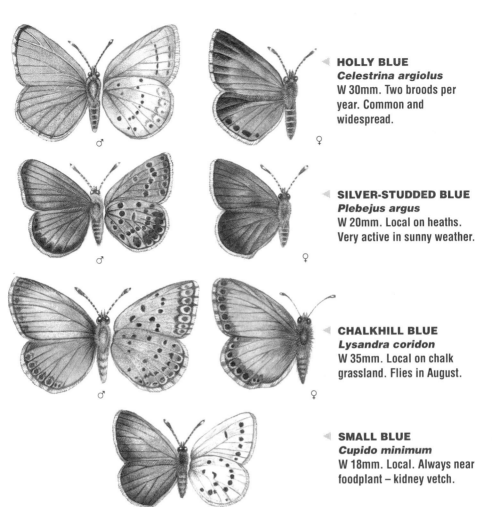

HOLLY BLUE
Celestrina argiolus
W 30mm. Two broods per
year. Common and
widespread.

♂ ♀

SILVER-STUDDED BLUE
Plebejus argus
W 20mm. Local on heaths.
Very active in sunny weather.

♂ ♀

CHALKHILL BLUE
Lysandra coridon
W 35mm. Local on chalk
grassland. Flies in August.

♂ ♀

SMALL BLUE
Cupido minimum
W 18mm. Local. Always near
foodplant – kidney vetch.

PROJECT

The caterpillars of chalkhill blue butterflies
are best discovered by searching
foodplants for excited groups of ants. The
caterpillars will be nearby, carefully
camouflaged. Sometimes the ants can be
seen climbing over the body of the
caterpillar. They are not attacking the larva
but rather collecting a sweet liquid
secreted by the caterpillar from special
glands. This behaviour is referred to as
'milking'. The ants protect the caterpillar
from parasitic wasps.

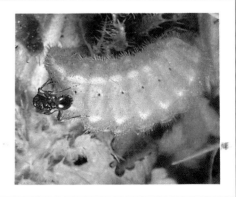

BUTTERFLIES

CHARACTERISTICS

The small copper and brown argus are unusual members of the 'blue' family of butterflies. Both have grub-like larvae. The skippers are active butterflies whose wings are held at an angle when they are at rest.

HABITS

The small copper is widespread wherever docks and sorrels – the larval foodplants – grow. It may have up to three broods in a year. Small coppers are active and seldom settle for long, except when feeding. The flight is fast and low. Skippers are active with a darting flight. They live in grasses, the larval foodplants.

The small copper is a very variable butterfly. The black spots on the forewing may be enlarged. Sometimes the orange band on the hind wing becomes a series of streaks. In var. *schmidtii* the orange becomes a pale tan.

The eggs of the small copper are laid on docks or sorrel. The caterpillar is extremely well camouflaged on its foodplant and difficult to locate. The chrysalis is attached to the plant by silk threads at the tail end.

SMALL COPPER
Lycaena phlaeas
W 25mm. Common and widespread. Meadows.

Learn to distinguish the Essex skipper (right) from the small skipper. These two species are extremely similar in appearance. They are both found in similar habitats – grassy meadows – and both can be seen on the wing in July and August. Small skippers and Essex skippers are very active little butterflies which flit and dart from flower to flower. The way to tell them apart is to look closely at the antennae. The underside of the tip in the small skipper is brown, whereas in the Essex skipper it is black. When they are feeding, or when resting in dull weather, this can be easy to spot.

DINGY SKIPPER ⏶
Erynnis tages
W 28mm. Rests with wings out flat. Flies in short bursts.

SMALL SKIPPER ⏶
Thymelicus flavus
W 25mm. Common in meadows. Active, 'buzzing' type of flight.

GRIZZLED SKIPPER ⏶
Pyrgus malvae
W 20mm. 'Buzzing' flight, low over ground. Locally common.

♂

♀

◀ **LARGE SKIPPER**
Ochlodes venatus
W 30mm. Common in meadows. Often seen feeding.

♂   ♀

◀ **BROWN ARGUS**
Articia agestis
W 25mm. Locally common in grassy places.

MOTHS

PRIVET HAWK MOTH
Sphinx ligustri
W 100mm. Common and widespread. Gardens and woodland edge.

Privet hawk moth eggs are laid on privet. The caterpillars are bright green and grow to a large size. When it is ready to pupate, the caterpillar buries itself in soil and forms a chamber.

CHARACTERISTICS

Hawk moths are large and spectacular species. The forewings are always much larger than the hind ones. Caterpillars usually have a horn-like projection at the tail end, and beautiful, diagonal stripes on each segment.

HABITS

They are sometimes found resting on walls or bark, especially when newly emerged from the chrysalis. Mating pairs may remain joined throughout the daytime. At night, hawk moths are sometimes seen on garden flowers. They feed on the wing, using the long proboscis to reach nectar. They are attracted to mercury-vapour-lamp moth traps. All are powerful fliers.

When at rest, eyed hawk moths resemble a dead leaf. If alarmed, they open their forewings to reveal striking eye markings on the hind-wings. This is likely to scare predators, such as birds.

ELEPHANT HAWK MOTH
Deilephila elepenor
W 70mm. Common and
widespread. Larvae feed
on willowherb.

PINE HAWK MOTH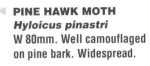
Hyloicus pinastri
W 80mm. Well camouflaged
on pine bark. Widespread.

POPLAR HAWK MOTH
Laothoe populi
W 70mm. Wings resemble
dry leaves. Larvae feed
on poplar.

DEATH'S HEAD HAWK MOTH
Acherontia atropos
W 120mm. Squeaks when
alarmed. Huge larvae feed
on potatoes.

MOTHS

CHARACTERISTICS

All the moths illustrated belong to the same family. The adult moths have downy bodies and wings. Prominents are so called because of the tufts of hairs on the hind edge of the wings.

HABITS

The moths show good camouflage when resting. Most resemble pieces of bark, but the buff tip looks like a broken-off birch twig. The striking caterpillars of the puss moth have two whip-like tail projections which arch and wave if the larva is alarmed. The head can also be contracted and swollen in defence.

The sallow kitten caterpillar pupates inside a cocoon attached to a branch. The protective cocoon is made of chewed bark and silk, and sets like cement. It is very hard to spot.

The female puss moth lays her eggs on willows. The caterpillar is easily identified and grows large. When ready to pupate, the larva chews the bark of the tree and combines this with silk to make a hard casing.

PUSS MOTH
Cerura vinula
W 70mm. Common and widespread near woodland and scrub.

LOBSTER MOTH
Stauropus fagi
W 55mm. Beech and oak woods. Larvae are lobster-like.

BUFF TIP ▷
Phalera bucephala
W 55mm. Rests with wings arched. Resembles wood chip.

SWALLOW PROMINENT
Pheosia tremula
W 50mm. Well camouflaged on bark. Common and widespread.

IRON PROMINENT ▷
Notodonta dromedarius
W 40mm. Common. Difficult to spot on bark. Comes to light.

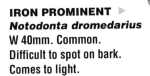

SALLOW KITTEN
Furcula furcula
W 35mm. Larvae resemble tiny puss moth larvae. Common.

MOTHS

CHARACTERISTICS

The cinnabar moth is mainly day-flying, but all species come readily to light after dark. In most species, the caterpillars are hairy; those of the garden tiger moth are called 'woolly-bears'. Cinnabar larvae have orange and black stripes.

HABITS

The garden tiger is a large and attractive species. Often attracted to lights, it may be found at the base of street lamps. The cinnabar moth and scarlet tiger are brightly coloured to warn of their unpleasant taste.

Garden tiger moths have forewings which are mottled brown and white. When resting, they mask the brightly-coloured hindwings. If alarmed, however, they are revealed to deter predators.

The eggs of the garden tiger are laid on a variety of low-growing plants. The favourite foods of the caterpillars are dandelion and dock. They pupate low down.

GARDEN TIGER MOTH
Arctia caja
W 65mm. Common and widespread. Gardens and rough ground.

CINNABAR MOTH ▼
Tyria jacobaeae
W 40mm. Common and widespread. Sometimes seen in daytime.

WHITE ERMINE ▲
Spilosoma lubricipeda
W 40mm. Common in fields. Comes to house lights.

COMMON FOOTMAN ▼
Eilema lurideola
W 48mm. Rests with wings flat. Scuttles when disturbed.

BUFF ERMINE ▲
Spilosoma lutea
W 40mm. Common in fields and meadows. Comes to house lights.

◀ **SCARLET TIGER MOTH**
Callimorpha dominula
W 45mm. Damp woodland. Flies on sunny days. Local.

PROJECT

Many insects, such as the caterpillar of the cinnabar moth, are brightly coloured. This makes them easy for birds and other predators to see, which might seem to be a disadvantage. However, the orange colour warns of the unpleasant taste of the larva, which is potentially poisonous to some animals. Look for the caterpillars, which are often seen on ragwort.

MOTHS

The heart and dart moth lays its eggs on chickweed and goosegrass. The caterpillars are brown, and pupate underground.

HEART AND DART
Agrotis exclamationis
W 32mm. Scuttles away when disturbed. Very common.

CHARACTERISTICS

The heart and dart and other moths illustrated are members of a group called noctuids. Their caterpillars are often hairless and plump.

HABITS

Like most noctuids, the heart and dart comes readily to light, even venturing indoors. Most noctuid caterpillars feed on almost any low-growing plant, and the moths are found in gardens, woods, fields and hedgerows. Most noctuids are dull, although large yellow and red underwings have, as their names suggest, got bright hindwings.

The herald moth is unusual because it hibernates through the winter. It is often found in sheds or garages; and several may congregate together in suitable spots.

THE HERALD ⏶
Scoliopteryx libatrix
W 40mm. Common in
gardens and parks.

LARGE YELLOW UNDERWING ⏶
Noctua pronuba
W 50mm. Common
everywhere. Rests on base
of plants during day.

SILVER-Y ⏶
Autographa gamma
W 38mm. Flies day and night.
Regular migrant to Britain.

PROJECT

Look for the Mother Shipton moth,
Callistege mi, W 35mm, a day-flying
species found in fields and woodland
rides. The name derives from the
curious markings on the forewings.
These are supposed to resemble the
profile of Mother Shipton, a renowned
witch. The moth flies during the early
summer and can be seen feeding on the
flowers of bugle and clover.

RED UNDERWING ⏶
Catocala nupta
W 70mm. Camouflaged
at rest. In open woodland
or parks.

MOTHS

CHARACTERISTICS

The lappet, drinker and lackey moths, which belong to the same family – Lasiocampidae – have hairy, plump bodies and hairy caterpillars. The yellowtail and black arches belong to a different family. The moths have slimmer bodies but they are also hairy.

HABITS

At rest, the wings of the lappet moth look like dry leaves. The caterpillars feed on hawthorn, and hibernate through the winter as young larvae. Yellowtail and black arches larvae are covered in irritating hairs.

The caterpillars of lackey moths live in colonies on bushes such as blackthorn. They build silk tents which help protect them from predators such as birds.

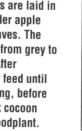

LAPPET MOTH
Gastropacha quercifolia
W 65mm. Common and widespread but easily overlooked. The males come to light. Hedgerows and woodland edges.

Lappet moth eggs are laid in small groups under apple and hawthorn leaves. The caterpillars vary from grey to reddish-brown. After hibernating, they feed until nearly 130mm long, before pupating in a silk cocoon attached to the foodplant.

THE LACKEY
Malacosoma neustria
W 30mm. Common along hedges. Larvae live in communal silk tents. Defoliate large areas.

YELLOWTAIL MOTH
Euproctis similis
W 40mm. Hedgerows and fields. All stages in life cycle have irritating hairs.

BLACK ARCHES
Lymantria monacha
W 40mm. Woodland. Well camouflaged on bark.

DRINKER MOTH
Philudoria potatoria
W 60mm. Found in ditches and damp meadows. Larvae drink water droplets.

MOTHS

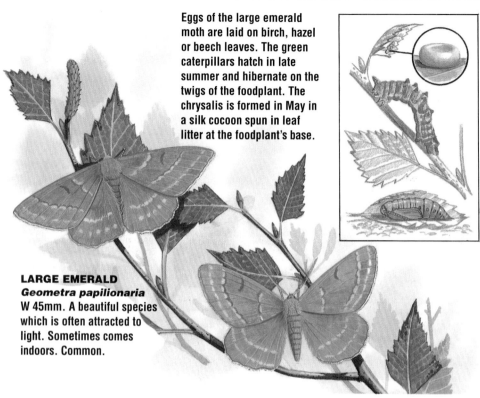

Eggs of the large emerald moth are laid on birch, hazel or beech leaves. The green caterpillars hatch in late summer and hibernate on the twigs of the foodplant. The chrysalis is formed in May in a silk cocoon spun in leaf litter at the foodplant's base.

LARGE EMERALD
Geometra papilionaria
W 45mm. A beautiful species which is often attracted to light. Sometimes comes indoors. Common.

CHARACTERISTICS

The large emerald, the swallowtail and the magpie moths all belong to a large family called the Geometridae. Their caterpillars are called 'loopers' because they move by looping-the-loop.

HABITS

When at rest, 'looper' larvae look like twigs. Some have coloured bumps which resemble young buds. Some geometrid moths are also camouflaged and look like dry leaves. The six-spot burnet belongs to a different family. Its squat caterpillar feeds on trefoils and pupates on grass stems. The adult moth's bright colours warn of its unpleasant taste.

The pupae of six-spot burnet moths are formed inside cocoons attached to grass stems. Pairs often mate soon after the female has emerged from the cocoon.

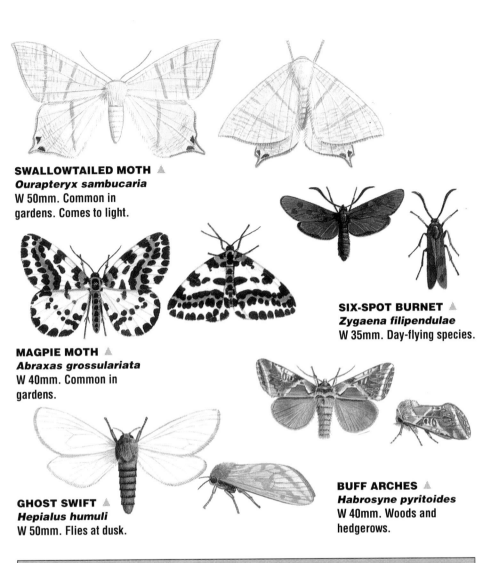

SWALLOWTAILED MOTH ▲
Ourapteryx sambucaria
W 50mm. Common in
gardens. Comes to light.

MAGPIE MOTH ▲
Abraxas grossulariata
W 40mm. Common in
gardens.

SIX-SPOT BURNET ▲
Zygaena filipendulae
W 35mm. Day-flying species.

GHOST SWIFT ▲
Hepialus humuli
W 50mm. Flies at dusk.

BUFF ARCHES ▲
Habrosyne pyritoides
W 40mm. Woods and
hedgerows.

PROJECT

Geometrid caterpillars are called 'loopers'
because of how they move. You can find
them among leaves and twigs in the
spring – hazel is good – or by using a
beating tray. Gently put a caterpillar on to
a bare twig. Watch how it moves: with the
back claspers gripping the stem, the body
is extended. With the front legs holding the
twig firmly, the claspers' grip is released
and the back of the body arches forward.

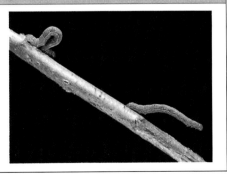

MICRO MOTHS

OAK LEAF ROLLER MOTH
Tortrix viridana
L 9mm. Common and widespread. Larva lives in rolled-up leaves. Moth is easily disturbed from

The oak leaf roller moth lays small groups of eggs on oak twigs. In spring, the caterpillars eat the buds, then feed on oak leaves, which they roll up with silk. They pupate in rolled leaves.

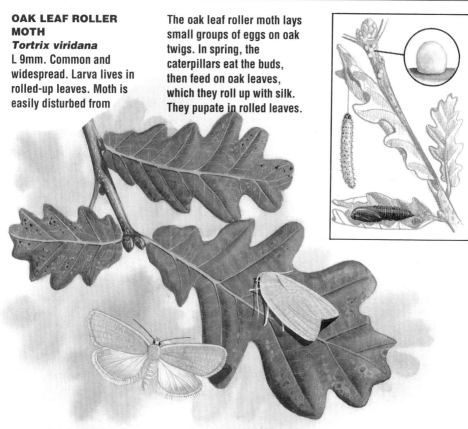

CHARACTERISTICS

Most of the moths that are seen regularly are quite large. However, there are also many which are considerably smaller and are collectively called micro moths. Although some are day-flying, most are nocturnal.

HABITS

Some micro moths are quite familiar because their caterpillars affect food and clothing. The larva of the clothes moth eats wool and other fabrics. Oak leaf roller moth larvae are common and are important as food for young birds.

The caterpillar of the codlin moth tunnels into apples and other fruit. Not only do the tunnels cause damage to the fruit itself but they also allow fungi and bacteria to attack the apple. The caterpillar is cream-white with a brown head. Unsprayed apples are attacked frequently.

How far do micro moth caterpillars travel? Moth caterpillars have three pairs of true legs and five pairs of false legs, which enable them to move at quite a speed. However, moving from branch to branch or reaching the ground can be a problem for species which feed on tree leaves. Several species of micro moth caterpillar have solved this in an ingenious way: they suspend themselves on silk threads and let the wind carry them until they reach another branch or leaf. Walk through a woodland in spring and you will see caterpillars dangling on silk threads. What is the longest thread you can see?

CHINA MARK MOTH ▷
Nymphula nymphaeata
W 25mm. Locally common near ponds and ditches. Larva is aquatic, living among weeds.

CLOTHES MOTH ▲
Tineola biselliella
L 8mm. Adult scuttles among clothes. Caterpillars eat holes in fabrics and furs.

CODLIN MOTH ▽
Cydia pomonella
L 10mm. Common and widespread. Always in the vicinity of fruit trees, especially apple.

◁ **WHITE PLUME MOTH**
Pterophorus pentadactyla
W 25mm. Common in hedges and fields. Comes to moth traps and lighted windows.

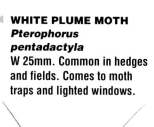

LONGHORN MOTH ▷
Adela reaumurata
L 9mm. Metallic wings. Males swarm around prominent, sunny branches of trees and bushes.

CADDISFLIES

CHARACTERISTICS

Caddisflies are common and widespread insects belonging to the order Trichoptera. Adults are moth-like but the wings are covered with hairs, not scales. They have long antennae.

HABITS AND HABITAT

Except for one rare species, the larvae always live in water. They construct clever tubular cases which protect their soft bodies. Some species use only plant matter to construct the case, others prefer grains of sand or small shells. A few live in silk webs, laid across the river, which catch food particles.

Limnephilus lunatus
L 15mm. Especially common in chalk streams and watercress beds.
1. Larva is soft-bodied apart from head, thorax and legs.
2. Stone and shell case.
3. Larva pupates inside the case.
4. Pupa escapes from case and climbs to water surface.
5. Adult emerges from pupa.
6. Adults mate and lay eggs.

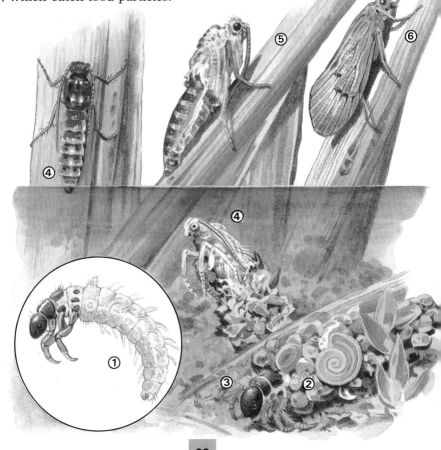

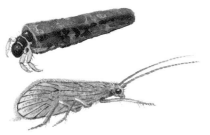

Brachycentrus ▲
subnubilis
L 12mm. Common in slow
rivers. Square cross-section
made of plant remains.

PROJECT

Most species of caddisfly larvae make
beautiful cases. If you want to watch the
building process in action, keep a few
larvae in a tank. *Limnephilus* larvae
make good subjects. Put sand and
small shells in the tank for them to use
to make their cases.

Anabolia nervosa ▲
L 15mm. Case of sand grains
with attached twigs. Streams
and clean ponds.

Hydropsyche pellucidula ▲
L 14mm. Ponds and slow
rivers. No case. Larva spins
webs among stones.

Phrygaena grandis ▲
L 30mm. Lakes and slow
rivers. Spiral case of
plant remains.

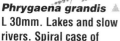

◄ **Triaenodes bicolor**
L 10mm. Common in lakes
and ponds. Spiral case of
leaf remains.

Agapetus fuscipes ▲
L 6mm. Very common in
stony streams. Sand and
gravel domed case.

TRUE FLIES

CHARACTERISTICS

The true flies illustrated belong to the order Diptera. This literally means 'two wings' – they fly using the front pair of wings only. The hindwings are much reduced and are generally club-shaped. They help the fly balance in flight.

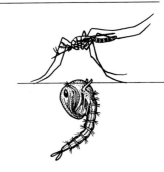

HABITS

Most adult flies feed on fluids and have mouthparts which assist this process. Some are like suction pipes whereas those of mosquitoes and horse flies are piercing. Fly larvae are very varied but are generally maggot-like. Although they may have well-developed mouthparts, the rest of the body lacks other conspicuous features of insects, such as legs.

Mosquito larvae live in water and are filter feeders. The pupae are also found in water. The adult insect emerges at the surface film, bursting through the skin of the pupa.

MOSQUITO
Aedes punctor
L 7mm. Common on heaths and in woods. Bites freely. Breeds in small pools.

BLACK FLY ▽
Simulium equinum
L 3mm. Female sucks
blood. Swarms around
horses and cattle.

BITING MIDGE △
Culex pipiens
L 6mm. Common. May breed
in water-storage tanks.
Seldom bites people.

ST MARK'S FLY ▽
Bibio marci
L 11mm. Common in spring.
Flies with dangling legs.

◁ **HORSE FLY**
Tabanus bromius
L 14mm. Females are
vicious biters. Fields
and woods.

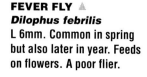

FEVER FLY △
Dilophus febrilis
L 6mm. Common in spring
but also later in year. Feeds
on flowers. A poor flier.

CRANE FLY △
Tipula paludosa
L 25mm. Common in
autumn. Leather-jacket
larvae in soil.

TRUE FLIES

CHARACTERISTICS

Hoverflies, robber flies and bee flies are all true flies. They fly using the front pair of wings. Hoverflies can hover in mid-air: their wings are a blur to our eyes, and many species make a loud buzzing sound as they hover.

HABITS

Hoverflies are often brightly coloured. The flies themselves are harmless but the markings often mimic wasps and bees, which puts off potential predators. Robber flies are fierce predators that attack and carry off other insects often as large as themselves. Bee flies look just like furry bumble bees. Their larvae live in bumble bee nests and eat bee larvae.

Drone flies have excellent eyesight with their large, compound eyes. They are often seen on flowers, feeding on nectar with their long sucking mouthparts. They particularly like flower heads of umbellifers.

DRONE FLY
Eristalis tenax
L 13mm. Common in gardens and woods. Eggs laid in water.

At first glance it can be very difficult to distinguish between a drone fly (far right) and the drone of a honey bee (left in picture). The fly mimics the bee as a means of defence. To tell the difference, look at the eyes and the wings. The drone fly's eyes are large and meet at the front of the head. Those of the bee are relatively smaller and do not meet. The fly has one pair of wings whereas the bee has a smaller second pair of wings.

BEE FLY ▷
Bombylius major
L 10mm. Found along sunny woodland glades in spring. Long proboscis distinctive.

HOVERFLY ▽
Volucella bombylans
L 14mm. Resembles a bumble bee. Feeds on flower heads and found in woods and gardens.

◁ **ROBBER FLY**
Asilius crabroniformis
L 24mm. Catches insects in mid-air. May use a regular look-out perch. Local.

◁ **HOVERFLY**
Volucella pellucens
L 14mm. Found in woodland rides and bramble patches.

HOVERFLY ▲
Syrphus ribesii
L 12mm. Common and widespread. Often seen on flower heads, feeding on nectar.

TRUE FLIES

CHARACTERISTICS

Like the flies illustrated previously, those here also fly using the two front wings, which are transparent and membranous. The hindwings are tiny stumps called *halteres*, which help stabilise the flight.

HABITS

Flies have a good sense of smell: house flies and bluebottles are often attracted to food inside houses. They lay their eggs on rotting flesh. The larvae develop quickly, eating the meat. Greenbottles seldom come indoors, preferring hedges. They may lay their eggs in wounds of cattle or sheep. Dung flies are attracted to cow and horse dung, which becomes covered with the orange-brown, males and mating pairs.

House flies have flexible mouthparts which act like a suction pump. The end is expanded and the flies can easily suck up fluids from flat surfaces. They are fond of substances such as damp food and jam.

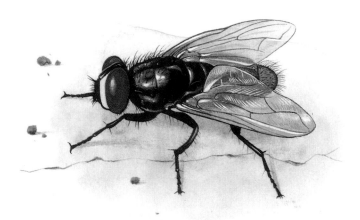

COMMON HOUSE FLY
Musca domestica
L 7mm. In and around houses and dustbins.
Common and widespread.

FLESH FLY
Sarcophaga carnaria
L 14mm. Common around habitation. Large feet and elongated body.

LESSER HOUSE FLY ▲
Fannia canicularis
L 5mm. Common in houses. Males fly constantly, usually just below ceiling.

GREENBOTTLE ▷
Lucilia caesar
L 9mm. Generally outdoors. Body has metallic sheen.

PROJECT

Most flies have an extremely keen sense of smell. Some species are attracted to rotting meat to feed and to lay eggs. Look for a curious fungus called the stinkhorn, which takes advantage of this. Its spores are contained in a sticky, foul- smelling jelly. Flies eat the jelly, and spread the spores when they fly away.

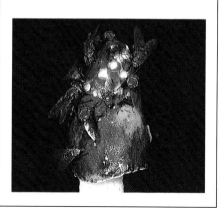

BLUEBOTTLE ▲
Calliphora vomitoria
L 11mm. Common in and around houses. Likes to sunbathe.

YELLOW DUNG FLY ▲
Scatophaga stercoraria
L 8mm. Males swarm on dung. Rather sluggish movement.

SAWFLIES

WOOD WASP OR HORNTAIL
Urocerus gigas
L 35mm. Fearsome but
harmless. Found in
pinewoods.

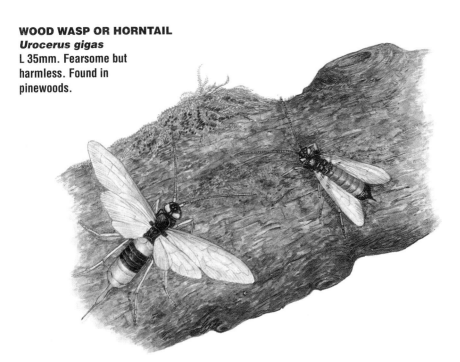

CHARACTERISTICS

Sawflies are related to bees, wasps and ants.
They have two pairs of membranous wings but
are poor fliers. The wings are held folded over
the back when they are at rest. Sawflies get
their name from the saw-like ovipositor which
females of some species use to lay eggs.

HABITS

Those species with well-developed ovipositors
lay their eggs inside plant stems. Other species
lay on leaves and buds. Sawfly larvae often
look rather like butterfly or moth caterpillars.
Almost all species feed on plant matter. Those
that live outside the plant eat leaves and
shoots, whereas species that live inside plants
eat the fibrous tissue.

The long needle-like
ovipositor of the female
wood wasp is surprisingly
strong. It is inserted into the
trunks of pine trees where
the eggs are deposited. The
larvae eat the tough tissue of
the tree and take three years
to develop. The larvae are
sometimes parasitised by an
ichneumon wasp.

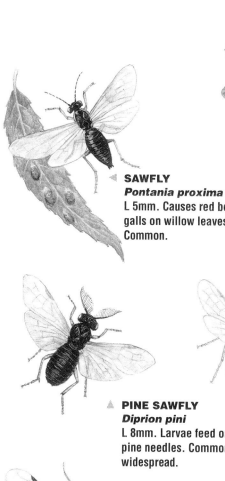

SAWFLY
Pontania proxima
L 5mm. Causes red bean galls on willow leaves. Common.

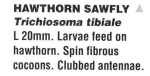

HAWTHORN SAWFLY
Trichiosoma tibiale
L 20mm. Larvae feed on hawthorn. Spin fibrous cocoons. Clubbed antennae.

GOOSEBERRY SAWFLY
Nematus ribesii
L 8mm. Larvae feed on and damage gooseberry and currant bushes.

PINE SAWFLY
Diprion pini
L 8mm. Larvae feed on pine needles. Common and widespread.

SAWFLY
Pamphilus sylvaticus
L 9mm. Larvae feed on hedgerow bushes. Adults fast-flying in sunny weather.

BIRCH SAWFLY
Cimbex femoratus
L 22mm. Larvae feed on birch leaves. Spin fibrous cocoons.

PROJECT

Learn how to recognise a sawfly larva. Many sawfly larvae look similar to the caterpillars of butterflies and moths. Both have three pairs of true legs near the head. However, caterpillars also have five pairs of false legs at the back, whereas most sawfly larvae have six or more pairs of false legs.

PARASITIC AND GALL WASPS

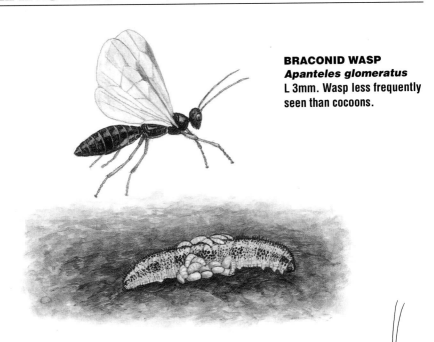

BRACONID WASP
Apanteles glomeratus
L 3mm. Wasp less frequently
seen than cocoons.

CHARACTERISTICS

Ichneumon, braconid and gall wasps are
related to bees and true wasps. Ichneumon
wasps have thin bodies with a narrow 'waist'.
Females may have long ovipositors. Gall wasps
are generally tiny insects and are seen much
less frequently than the galls that they cause.

HABITS

Female ichneumons use their ovipositors to lay
eggs inside other insects. Ichneumon larvae live
inside the body. They do not kill it straight
away, but eat the body gradually, using it as a
food store. Female gall wasps lay eggs in plant
tissue, often causing it to swell and grow into
strange shapes. Gall wasp larvae are often
parasitised by ichneumon wasps.

The eggs of the ichneumon
wasps are laid in the host's
body. A long, sharp
ovipositor is inserted through
the skin of the insect or
spider. Larvae and pupae are
particularly vulnerable. The
whole operation of egg-
laying is extremely quick and
is finished in an instant.

Many ichneumon and braconid wasps are small and difficult to spot. Some can be seen on flower heads in summer but the best way to see them is to collect a parasitised caterpillar. Look for the tell-tale cocoons attached to the body. Keep the caterpillar until the wasps emerge from it.

ROBIN'S PINCUSHION GALL WASP ▲
Diplolepis rosae
L 5mm. Gall 25mm across. Found on wild roses. Male wasps very rare.

ICHNEUMON WASP ▲
Rhyssa persuasoria
L 25mm. Fairly common in pine woods, where it parasitises horntail larvae.

SPANGLE GALL WASP ▽
Neuroterus quercusbaccarum
L 2mm. Gall 3mm across. On underside of oak leaves.

MARBLE GALL WASP ▲
Andricus kollari
L 6mm. Gall 18mm across. Spherical galls on oak; green then brown. Round exit hole.

OAK APPLE GALL WASP ▲
Biorhiza pallida
L 3mm. Gall 30mm across. Found on oak twigs.

ANTS AND POTTER WASPS

WOOD ANT
Formica rufa
L 10mm. Large colonial
mounds found in woodland.

CHARACTERISTICS

Ants are social insects that live in colonies.
They are related to bees, wasps and sawflies.
Ants have a narrow 'waist' between the
thorax and abdomen.

HABITS

Most ants in a colony are wingless workers.
During the summer, winged males and queens
form mating swarms which eventually form
new colonies. Ants are very fierce. Although
they cannot sting, they have powerful
mouthparts and can spray formic acid at
intruders. The eggs, larvae and pupae of the
ants are cared for in the underground nest.
Some species, such as wood ants, feed on other
insects and kill large numbers of pests. Others
collect organic debris or seeds. Ants have
sensitive antennae, which are used to detect
food, to follow trails and to communicate
with each other.

Wood ants are very strong.
They can overpower insects
many times their own size.
These are then dragged to
the nest mound where they
are dismembered and often
fed to the growing larvae.
Watch a trail of ants
returning to the colony and
you will see a range of
their victims.

Some ants, such as the black ant, have a special relationship with aphids. They collect the sweet honeydew from the aphids and in return protect them from predators such as ladybirds and their larvae. Almost any group of blackfly (aphids) will have ants in attendance, and they may even be held in the nest to provide an immediate supply of honeydew. Watch closely to see the ants collecting droplets of honeydew from the tip of the aphid's abdomen.

RUBY-TAILED WASP ▽
Chrysis ignita
L 10mm. Seen on walls and tree trunks. Metallic sheen.

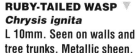

RED ANT △
Myrmica rubra
L 4mm. Common in garden soil. Often nests under paving stones.

PAPER WASP △
Polistes gallicus
L 22mm. Builds suspended nest in sheds. Not in Britain.

POTTER WASP ▷
Eumenes coarctatus
L 14mm. Common on heathland. Builds vase-shaped nest.

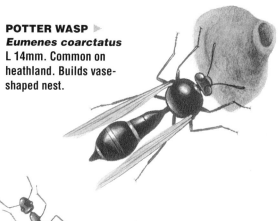

DIGGER WASP △
Ammophila sabulosa
L 20mm. Found in sandy areas. Egg laid on paralysed caterpillar in burrow nest.

◁ **BLACK ANT**
Lasius niger
L 4mm. Common in gardens. Nests under paving stones.

WASPS

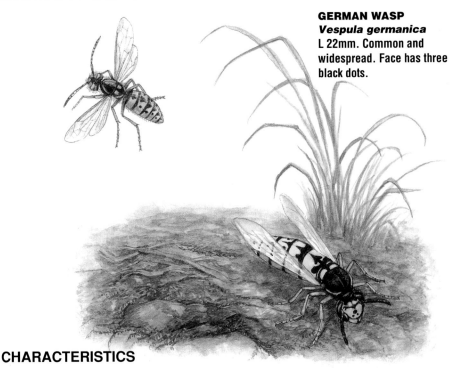

GERMAN WASP
Vespula germanica
L 22mm. Common and
widespread. Face has three
black dots.

CHARACTERISTICS

Most wasp species are colonial insects that fly using two unequal pairs of transparent wings. Some have powerful stings to protect themselves and disable other insects. Unlike bees, wasps do not die after they have used their stings.

HABITS

Wasps make their nests in hollow trees and often in the roofs of houses. Nests are built of paper made from chewed wood. Small cells are constructed in which the eggs are laid and later the larvae are reared. Adult wasps feed on nectar and fruit, and collect caterpillars to feed to their larvae. Digger wasps and field digger wasps nest in burrows in sandy soil. These are stocked with paralysed insects, which are food for the larvae.

Wasps love to feed on fruit. In the autumn, windfall apples provide a feeding bonanza. If the apples begin to rot, the wasps are attracted in great numbers. Watch their powerful mouthparts being used to bite large chunks of fruit. If the apples ferment, the wasps become sluggish after feeding.

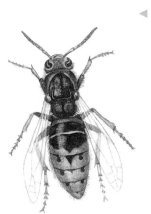

HORNET
Vespa crabro
L 35mm. Large and fearsome. Nests in old trees or houses

COMMON WASP ▷
Vespula vulgaris
L 23mm. Face with club-shaped black line, not dots. Common. Often nests in houses.

NORWEGIAN WASP ▲
Vespula norvegica
L 22mm. Face with vertical black line, not dots. Common and widespread.

PROJECT

Wasps defend their nests vigorously during the summer months and these should never be approached too closely. If you have a nest in your roof or an outhouse, winter is the time to examine it. All the wasps except the queen will have died and she will be hibernating elsewhere. You will see sheets made of hexagonal paper chambers in which the larvae lived.

DIGGER WASP ▲
Crabro cribrarius
L 12mm. Common in sandy areas. Powerful front legs. Can be seen carrying paralysed insects.

FIELD DIGGER WASP ▲
Mellinus arvensis
L 12mm. Found in sandy areas. Drags paralysed insects.

BEES

BUFF-TAILED BUMBLE BEE
Bombus terrestris
L 25mm. Common and
widespread. Workers and
males smaller.

CHARACTERISTICS

Bees belong to the order Hymenoptera. This literally means 'membrane-wings' and refers to their delicate, transparent wings – they fly using two pairs. Most bees are colonial.

HABITS

Bumble bees form new colonies each year, usually in holes – they may be abandoned mouse burrows. Only the queen survives the winter. In the spring and summer, she produces males and workers, which help raise the colony's brood. Man encourages honey bee colonies to live in hives so that honey can easily be removed regularly. They can communicate with each other: at the hive they perform a 'dance' telling others where to fly.

A bee's head shows the well-developed compound eyes and antennae. The mouthparts are perfectly suited to feeding on flowers. They can be inserted deep into the flower heads to reach the source of nectar.

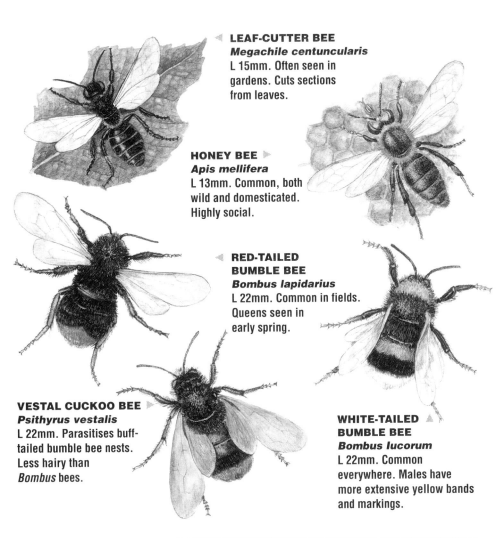

LEAF-CUTTER BEE
Megachile centuncularis
L 15mm. Often seen in gardens. Cuts sections from leaves.

HONEY BEE
Apis mellifera
L 13mm. Common, both wild and domesticated. Highly social.

RED-TAILED BUMBLE BEE
Bombus lapidarius
L 22mm. Common in fields. Queens seen in early spring.

VESTAL CUCKOO BEE
Psithyrus vestalis
L 22mm. Parasitises buff-tailed bumble bee nests. Less hairy than *Bombus* bees.

WHITE-TAILED BUMBLE BEE
Bombus lucorum
L 22mm. Common everywhere. Males have more extensive yellow bands and markings.

HOW TO WATCH

Wild bee nests are difficult to observe because they are usually in hollow trees. However, domesticated bees are more easy to see. If you know someone who keeps bees, ask whether you can watch when they collect the honey or clean the hive. You will see hexagonal chambers in which the bees store honey, or lay eggs and raise their larvae.

WATER BEETLES

CHARACTERISTICS

Dip a net into a pond or weedy lake and you will find water beetles. Like their land relatives, their front wings are hardened to protect the hindwings. Some species have flattened hind legs, fringed with hairs, which help to propel their streamlined bodies.

HABITS

Although they live in water, water beetles do not have gills. They breathe air, and some of them carry air with them to stay longer under water. This is trapped in hairs on the body or held under the wing cases. Most water beetles fly well and can travel long distances after dark to find a new pond.

Water beetle larvae also live in water. In order to breathe, the great diving beetle larva has a fringe of hairs around the tip of the abdomen. These make contact with the surface film of the water.

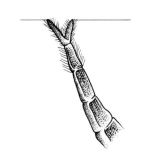

SILVER WATER BEETLE
Hydrophilus piceus
L 40mm. Silvery in water owing to trapped air. Sometimes seen replenishing air at surface.

WHIRLYGIG BEETLE ▽
Gyrinus natator
L 6mm. Active at water
surface. Dives readily.

GREAT DIVING BEETLE △
Dytiscus marginalis
L 30mm. Large and active
predator. Renews air supply
with abdomen at surface.

WATER BEETLE △
Acilius sulcatus
L 18mm. Found in ponds and
lakes. Beautiful sculptured
markings on wing cases.

SCREECH BEETLE △
Hygrobia hermanni
L 9mm. Found in pond and
lakes. Squeaks when
alarmed or handled.

PROJECT

Water beetles do not have gills like
damselfly and mayfly nymphs. Instead
they have to return to the water's
surface to breathe air. You can
sometimes see a great diving beetle
with the tip of its abdomen at the
surface. It is replenishing the air store
which is kept underneath its wing
cases. This is often easier to observe by
catching the beetle and putting it in a
tank. Remember to release it later.

LAND BEETLES

CHARACTERISTICS

Beetles are a varied group of insects. More species live on land than in water and they are usually very active. Beetles generally have powerful, biting mouthparts. The front pair of wings in most beetles are hardened and form wing cases – *elytra* – that protect the folded hindwings used for flying.

HABITS

Many species are carnivorous but some feed on plants or decaying matter. Larvae are usually grub-like. Some live in soil, while others live under bark or in rotting wood. The burying beetle larva feeds on the corpse of a small mammal or bird, buried by the adult beetles. Glow-worm larvae feed on snails.

Male stag beetles use their antler-shaped jaws to battle with each other. The winner, which is the stronger of the two combatants, mates with any nearby females. Although these fights may look fierce, the beetles are seldom damaged.

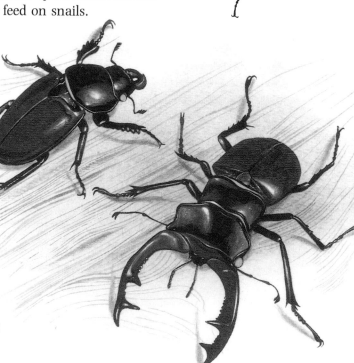

STAG BEETLE
Lucanus cervus
L 40mm. Found in old woodland. Larvae live in rotting trunks.

ROSE CHAFER ▽
Cetonia aurata
L 20mm. Feeds on flowers.
Especially fond of roses.

VIOLET GROUND BEETLE ▽
Carabus violaceus
L 25mm. Shiny body. Very
active but hides in crevices
during daytime.

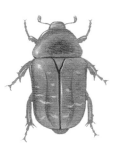

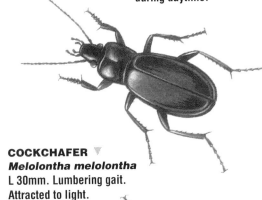

COCKCHAFER ▽
Melolontha melolontha
L 30mm. Lumbering gait.
Attracted to light.

CARDINAL BEETLE ▽
Pyrochroa coccinea
L 15mm. Conspicuous on
flowers and tree stumps.
Found in mature woodland.

BURYING BEETLE
Necrophorus vespilloides
L 18mm. Found under
carcasses. Sometimes
attracted to light.

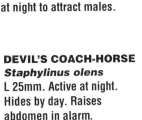

GLOW-WORM ▷
Lampyris noctiluca
L 12mm. Found in meadows
and hedges. Females glow
at night to attract males.

DEVIL'S COACH-HORSE
Staphylinus olens
L 25mm. Active at night.
Hides by day. Raises
abdomen in alarm.

LAND BEETLES

CHARACTERISTICS

The species here illustrate the wide range of shape and form found among beetles. Most have the forewings hardened to form wing cases. However, the oil beetle has reduced wing cases and is flightless.

Oil beetles have a curious life cycle. Young larvae climb up flowers and cling to bees. These carry them back to their nest, where the larva grows feeding on honey.

HABITS

Like other longhorn beetles, the larvae of the wasp beetle live inside rotting wood and bore tunnels. Oil beetle larvae live in the nests of solitary bees. The bloody-nosed beetle is also flightless and has the wing cases fused together. Both adult and larval ladybirds feed on aphids.

WASP BEETLE
Clytus arietis
L 20mm. Feeds on flower heads. Mimics wasps in behaviour as well as in appearance.

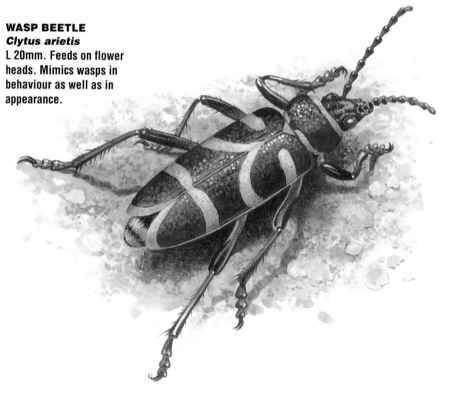

FURNITURE BEETLE ▽
Anobium punctatum
L 4mm. Widespread in houses.

SEVEN-SPOT LADYBIRD ▽
Coccinella 7-punctata
L 6mm. Commonest ladybird. Often on roses in gardens.

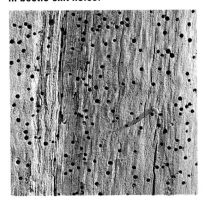
◀ BLOODY-NOSED BEETLE
Timarcha tenebricosa
L 17mm. Local in grassland. Exudes red fluid when alarmed. Lumbering gait.

OIL BEETLE ▽
Meloe proscarabeus
L 25mm. Meadows. Releases an oily fluid when alarmed.

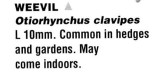

WEEVIL ▲
Otiorhynchus clavipes
L 10mm. Common in hedges and gardens. May come indoors.

AQUATIC LARVAE

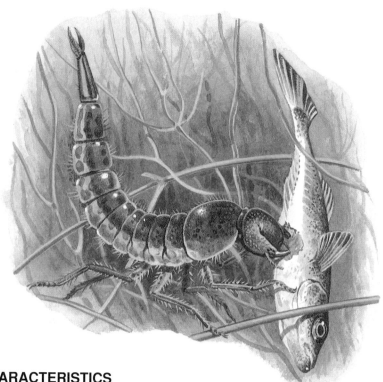

CHARACTERISTICS

Many insect larvae live in water, whereas the adults are terrestrial. Some use gills to absorb oxygen in the water. Others return to the water's surface to breathe air. Damselfly nymphs have three, flattened, gills. Mayfly nymphs have gills along the abdomen, whereas rat-tailed maggots have breathing tubes that reach the water's surface.

HABITS

Diving beetle larvae and dragonfly and mayfly nymphs move actively through water. Damselfly nymphs and fly larvae are more sluggish. Caddisfly larvae build cases.

DIVING BEETLE LARVA
Dytiscus marginalis
L 45mm. Common in ponds and canals. Fierce predator.

Diving beetle
This larva is a ferocious predator and will attack small fish and tadpoles without hesitation. The sharp mandibles pierce the skin of the victim, which is then literally sucked dry. It is a greenish-brown colour, which helps to camouflage it among weeds.

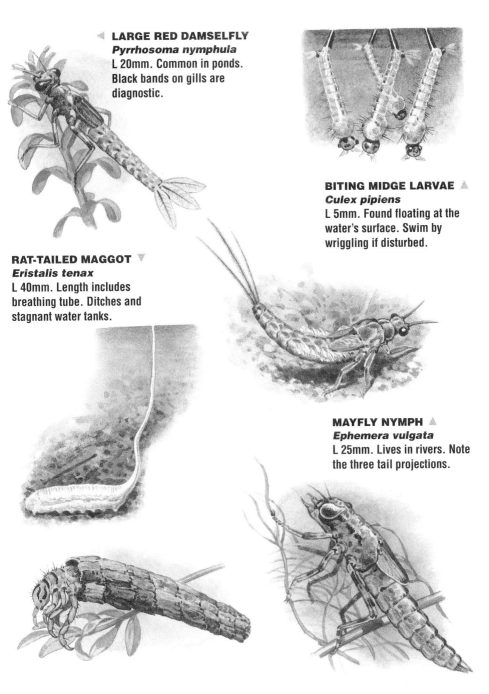

LARGE RED DAMSELFLY
Pyrrhosoma nymphula
L 20mm. Common in ponds. Black bands on gills are diagnostic.

BITING MIDGE LARVAE ▲
Culex pipiens
L 5mm. Found floating at the water's surface. Swim by wriggling if disturbed.

RAT-TAILED MAGGOT ▼
Eristalis tenax
L 40mm. Length includes breathing tube. Ditches and stagnant water tanks.

MAYFLY NYMPH ▲
Ephemera vulgata
L 25mm. Lives in rivers. Note the three tail projections.

CADDISFLY LARVA ▲
Limnephilus lunatus
L 25mm. Builds an intricate case of twigs and sand.

EMPEROR DRAGONFLY NYMPH ▲
Anax imperator
L 50mm. Active predator. Common in larger ponds.

TERRESTRIAL LARVAE

CHARACTERISTICS

Some of the insects that you find in the course of your studies will be larvae and not adults. It may be difficult to identify the species but you should be able to work out to which order of insects they belong. The caterpillars of moths and butterflies are the most widely encountered larvae.

DIFFERENT TYPES

Some caterpillars look quite unlike ordinary species so study them carefully. If you want to identify the species precisely, collect it and rear it through to the adult stage, feeding it on the plant it was found on. Most fly larvae live hidden away but some, such as the hoverfly larva, are free-living and are fierce predators.

The caterpillars of the garden tiger moth are hairy. These irritate the skin and mouths of predators. When disturbed, the caterpillars roll into a ball so the entire body is protected by the hairs.

HOVERFLY LARVA
Syrphus balteatus
L 7mm. Feeds on aphids. Common in gardens and hedgerows.

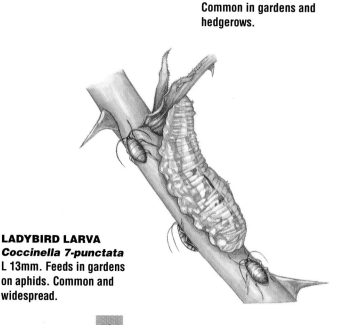

LADYBIRD LARVA
Coccinella 7-punctata
L 13mm. Feeds in gardens on aphids. Common and widespread.

MEADOW BROWN ▷
Maniola jurtina
L 14mm. Common in
meadows. Feeds on grasses
at night but hides at ground
level by day.

GOOSEBERRY SAWFLY ▲
Nematus ribesii
L 8mm. Common in gardens.
Large groups often found.
Can strip whole bushes.

COCKCHAFER LARVA ▼
Melolontha melolontha
L 50mm. Lives buried in soil.
Eats roots, causing damage.

ELEPHANT HAWK MOTH ▲
Deilephila elpenor
L 50mm. Feeds on
willowherb. 'Eyes' swell
when alarmed.

LARGE WHITE CATERPILLAR ▷
Pieris brassicae
L 30mm. Pest of cabbages.
Often in large groups.

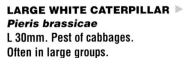

INDEX

ILLUSTRATIONS BY

Bernard Thornton Artists: Robert Morton 98–99, 120–123 · Folio: Janet Duff 26 · The Gallery: Isabel Bowring 12–13, 18–25, 48–49, 66–83 · Garden Studios: Shirley Felts cover · Ian Flemming Associates: Miranda Grey 7, 10–11, 16–17, 124–125 · Karen Johnson 20–21 (top centre), 46–47 (top right), 55 (top right), 79 (lower centre) · John Martin Artists: Tricia Newell 46–47, 52–55, 58–59, 62–63, 100–101, 106–109, 112–115 · Linden Artists: Alan Male 14–15, 50–51, 56–57, 60–61, 64–65, 102–105, 110–111, 116–119; Phil Weare 4–5, 28–43 · Maltings Partnership 6–7 · Chris Shields 84–97. Additional black and white line illustrations by Karen Johnson.

The Publishers would like to thank the following organisations and individuals for their kind permission to reproduce the photographs in this book.

Nature Photographers: Front Cover; S C Bisserot 5 below, 117; Frank Blackburn 74; K Blamire 58; Chris Brown 57; Nicholas Brown 16, 62; Robin Bush 27 centre, 61; N A Callow 11 centre, 64, 80; Andrew Cleave 41, 92, 107; Ron Croucher 59; C H Gomersall 9; Jean Hall 105; L G Jessup 49; Don Smith 72; Paul Sterry 5 above, 7 below, 11 above & below, 13, 17, 25, 26, 27, 31, 35, 39, 43, 52, 65, 69, 73, 75, 81, 83, 84, 86, 88, 89, 90, 91, 94, 95, 97, 99, 102, 103, 109, 111, 112, 113, 115, 121, 124; Anthony Wharton 78 · NHPA: Stephen Dalton 21 · Swift Picture Library: Robin Fletcher 37